THE CANADIAN PRESS

CAPS AND SPELLING

21ST EDITION
Fully revised and updated

James McCarten, Editor

THE CANADIAN PRESS
36 King St. East, Toronto, Ontario M5C 2L9

www.thecanadianpress.com

Library and Archives Canada Cataloguing in Publication

CP caps and spelling
       The Canadian Press caps and spelling / James McCarten,
editor. – 21st edition.

Editions 1-19 edited by Patti Tasko.
ISBN 978-0-920009-52-9 (paperback)

       1. English language–Capitalization. 2. English language–
Orthography and spelling. I. McCarten, James, 1969-, editor
II. Canadian Press, issuing body III. Title. IV. Title: Caps and
spelling.

PE1450.C72 2015   423'.1   C2015-905586-5

First printing 1965 Revised 1969, 1973, 1976, 1978, 1981, 1985,
1986, 1987, 1988, 1990, 1992, 1996, 1998, 2000, 2003, 2005, 2007,
2009, 2012 and 2015.

Design and cover art by
Sean Vokey
The Canadian Press

Foreword

It began life in 1965 as a slim, wire-bound compendium of words, proper names and abbreviations, designed to provide "ready reference on the desk as distinguished from the detailed study necessary to absorb the contents of the *CP Style Book.*"

Fifty years later, times have changed. Stylebook, for instance, is one word. Journalism is no longer confined to yellowing newsprint. And to refer generically to newsroom staff members as "deskmen," as the opening paragraphs of *Caps* did a half-century ago, would elicit a fearsome rebuke from any self-respecting editor, to say nothing of the Canadian public.

As the years have ticked by, the content has evolved.

In 1965, Nike was a missile, not a multinational. Dolor has disappeared, replaced by do-not-call list. Long gone is the Loop, making room for Lycra and Lyme disease. ICBM has given way to IED.

Modern media outlets no longer shy away from reporting on suicide to the extent they once did, but it's a subject that demands care and sensitivity. In this edition of *Caps and Spelling*, The Canadian Press is discouraging the use of the expression 'committed suicide,' and also making it clear that 'assisted suicide' and 'assisted death' are interchangeable, acceptable terms when writing about palliative care and end-of-life issues.

Some things, of course, never change. There is still no B in numskull, and only two Ls in skilful. It's oilsands, not tarsands, as was the case 50 years ago (although in those days, it was two words). And 'postpone until later' is still a redundancy, even if it's no longer in the book.

Foreword

After a half-century of evolution, the defining objective of the 21st edition of *Caps and Spelling* remains the same as the first: bringing together the proper names and abbreviations most likely to cause problems for those handling copy in Canadian newsrooms.

In this edition, many listings have been updated or removed and new ones added,including: 60s Scoop, 4-20 (for April 20 'Weed Day'), blue line, Al Jazeera, Bitcoin and bitcoins, BlackBerry, Bridle Path, Canadian Security Establishment, Hillary Rodham Clinton, commissioner, income splitting and income-splitting policy, Irbil, Islamic State of Iraq and the Levant, ISIL, Jos. Louis, Kolkata, Lac-Megantic, locker room, Martin Luther King Jr. Day, Much (formerly MuchMusic), Much Music Video Awards, OCAD University, Queens Quay, Re/Max, Redblacks, Sunshine List, Toronto Eaton Centre, al-Shabab, assisted suicide, assisted death, bobblehead, committed suicide, crowdsourcing, crowdfunding, developing nations, doctor-assisted suicide, doctor-assisted death, dwarf, e-cigarette, endgame, flashpoint, goal line, guardrail, iCloud, live-blog, live-blogging, micronutrient, new veterans charter, opiate, opioid, overbilling, parliamentary budget officer and Office of the Parliamentary Budget Officer, red line, ride-hailing, ride-booking, spinarama, suicide, temporary foreign workers, vape, vaping and vape pen, weekday, weekend, weeklong, work-to-rule campaign.

This 21st edition is the third to be published since *Caps and Spelling* moved online. Both *Caps* and the *Stylebook* now are available online; subscribers to the Internet version have already received the updates and additions in this book. If you are interested in

Foreword

real-time updates and email notifications of all style changes or additional content in our books, visit thecanadianpress.com/books.

Many of the changes and additions to *Caps and Spelling* come at the request of the writers and editors who use the *Canadian Press Stylebook* and this book. Thanks, as always, go to those alert and loyal users who continue to help in keeping this reference up to date.

James McCarten, Editor

james.mccarten@thecanadianpress.com

Capitalization

1. The Canadian Press follows a modified down style. This is the basic rule:

Capitalize all proper names, the names of departments and agencies of national and provincial governments, trade names, names of associations, companies, clubs, religions, languages, races, places, addresses. Otherwise, lowercase is favoured where a reasonable option exists.

2. Common nouns — church, league — are capitalized when part of a proper name: Anglican Church, National Hockey League. They are normally lowercased when standing alone: the church's stand, a league spokesman.

3. The common-noun elements of proper nouns are normally lowercase in plural uses: the United and Anglican churches, the National and American leagues.

4. Formal titles directly preceding a name are capitalized: Prime Minister Stephen Harper, Archbishop Tom Collins. They are lowercased standing alone and in plural uses: the prime minister, the archbishop, premiers Jean Charest and Dalton McGuinty.

5. As a rule of thumb, formal titles are those that are almost an integral part of a person's name — they could be used with the surname alone, if that were Canadian Press style: Ald. Cowan, Rabbi Steinberg, Sgt. Duplessis.

6. Job descriptions are lowercased: soprano Maria Stratas, managing editor Anne Davies, Acme Corp. chairman Joseph Schultz.

7. Long or cumbersome titles and job descriptions should be set off with commas: Jean Dubois, energy, mines and resources minister, attended. Or: The energy, mines and resources minister, Jean Dubois, attended. An internationally known Canadian writer, Alice Munro, was present.

8. All references to the current Pope, Canada's reigning monarch and the current Governor General are capitalized.

9. Titles of nobility, religion and suchlike that are commonly used instead of the personal name are capitalized: Duke of Kent, Anglican Primate of Canada. But the duke, the primate.

10. The names of national legislative bodies, including some short forms, are capitalized: House of Commons, the House, the Commons; U.S. Senate; Knesset. Provincial legislatures and local councils are lowercased: Quebec national assembly, Toronto city council.

11. National and provincial government departments and agencies are capitalized: Health Canada, Defence Department, Ministry of Natural Resources, U.S. Secret Service. Local government departments and boards are lowercased: parks and property department, Halifax welfare department.

12. Upper courts are capitalized: B.C. Supreme Court, Appeal Court. Lower courts are lowercased: juvenile court, magistrate's court.

13. Canada's military forces are capitalized: Canadian Forces, the Forces. For other forces, army, navy and air force are lowercased when preceded by the name of the country: the Greek air force, the U.S. army. This style is intended for consistency since the proper

Capitalization

name is not always a combination of country and force: the Royal Navy, the British navy; the Royal Air Force, the British air force.

14. Historical periods, historic events, holy days and other special times are capitalized: Middle Ages, First World War, Prohibition, Christmas Eve, Ramadan, Earth Day, October Crisis.

15. Specific geographical regions and features are capitalized: Western Canada, Far North, Lake Superior, Niagara Peninsula. But northern, southern, eastern and western in terms derived from regions are lowercased: a western Canadian, a southerner, northern customs.

16. Regions not generally known as specific geographical areas are lowercase: southern Ontario, eastern Alberta, northern Newfoundland.

17. Sacred names and the proper names and nicknames of the devil are capitalized: the Almighty, Redeemer, Holy Spirit, Allah, Mother of God, Vishnu, Beelzebub, Father of Lies. But devil, hell and heaven are lowercased.

18. Names of races, nations and the like are capitalized: Aboriginal Peoples, Asian, Arab, French-Canadian. But white and black are lowercased.

19. The principal words of titles of books, plays, movies, paintings and the like are capitalized: *A Dictionary of Usage and Style, Androcles and the Lion, Gone With the Wind, Isle of the Dead*. Principal words are nouns, pronouns, adjectives, adverbs, verbs, the first and last word of the title, as well as prepositions and conjunctions of four letters or more. For infinitives, use to Go, to Be. Both words of compound adjectives are capitalized: Well-Meaning.

20. Nicknames and fanciful names are capitalized: Speedy Gonzales, Mack the Knife, Third World, Group of Seven.

21. Awards and decorations are capitalized: Order of Canada, OC; Victoria Cross, VC. University degrees are lowercased except when abbreviated: master of arts, a master's, MA; doctor of philosophy, PhD.

22. Proper nouns and adjectives now regarded as common nouns are lowercased: brussels sprouts, french fries, draconian, scotch.

23. Except in the cases of all-lowercase or all-uppercase names, follow the capitalization used by the organization or person unless it hampers readability: eBay, iPod, WestJet, k.d. lang. Note: Capitalize at the beginning of a sentence: EBay. If a corporate or promotional name is all lowercase, cap the first letter for clarity: Adidas. If the name is all uppercase, cap only the first letter for readability: Band-Aid (not BAND-AID). Some exceptions to these rules may be necessary for readability; they will be listed in this book.

For a fuller treatment of capitalization, see the Canadian Press Stylebook, chapter Capitalization.

Spelling

1. The *Canadian Oxford Dictionary* is the authority for Canadian Press spelling with specific exceptions noted in the *Canadian Press Stylebook* and this guide. Where optional forms are given — moustache, mustache — the first listed is Canadian Press style.

2. When the spelling of the common-noun element of a proper name differs from Canadian Press style — Center Harbor, N.H., Lincoln Center, Canadian Paediatric Society — use the spelling favoured by the subject.

3. The Canadian Press ignores symbols and unnecessary punctuation in corporate or other names or translates them into accepted punctuation if necessary: 'N Sync, not *NSYNC; Yahoo Inc., not Yahoo! Inc.; Mamma Mia, not Mamma Mia! Check individual listings.

4. Canadian Press style is -our, not -or, for labour, honour and other such words of more than one syllable in which the "u" is not pronounced:

arbour	ardour	armour
behaviour	candour	clamour
clangour	colour	demeanour
discolour	dishonour	enamour
endeavour	favour	fervour
flavour	glamour	harbour
honour	humour	labour
neighbour	odour	parlour
rancour	rigour	rumour
saviour	savour	splendour
tumour	valour	vapour
vigour		

5. In some forms of these words, however, the "u" is dropped, especially when an -ous ending is added: laborious, rancorous, odorous, honorary.

6. Canadian Press style also reflects "Canadian" spellings that are different from American spellings. Some examples (American form in brackets):

axe (ax)	catalogue (catalog)
centre (center)	cheque (check)
defence (defense)	enrol (enroll)
grey (gray)	ketchup (catsup)
licence (n.) (license)	litre (liter)
manoeuvre (maneuver)	meagre (meager)
metre (meter)	mould (mold)
moustache (mustache)	offence (offense)
pedlar (peddler)	skilful (skillful)
sombre (somber)	spectre (specter)
syrup (sirup)	theatre (theater)
pyjamas (pajamas)	

As well, Canadian Press and Canadian style is usually to double the l when adding endings to words such as label and signal. American spelling tends to leave it as a single l.

7. For words in common use, Canadian Press style is simple "e" rather than the diphthongs "ae" and "oe." Thus Canadian Press style is archeologist, ecumenical, encyclopedia, esthetic, fetus, gynecologist, hemorrhage, medieval, paleontologist, pedagogy and pediatrician.

8. Generally, proper names retain the diphthong: Caesar, Oedipus, Phoebe. Also hors d'oeuvre, manoeuvre and subpoena. The "ae" in aerial, aerate and such is considered normal spelling.

Spelling

9. The umlaut — ä, ö and ü — in German names is indicated by the letter "e" after the letter affected. Thus: Goering for Göring.

10. The -ov and -ev endings for Russian names are used instead of -off and -eff. Exceptions include such familiar names as Rachmaninoff, Smirnoff and Ignatieff, where the spelling is established.

11. Canadian Press style for First Nations names is to follow the preference of the band. For a current list of bands and their preferred spellings, check the First Nations Profiles page on the website of Aboriginal Affairs and Northern Development Canada (http://www.aadnc-aandc.gc.ca/).

12. For Arabic names, use an English spelling that approximates the way a name sounds in Arabic. If an individual has a preferred spelling in English, use it.

13. Use the Ukrainian, not the Russian, transliteration for Ukrainian place names: Chornobyl (not Chernobyl); Kyiv (not Kiev).

Abbreviations

1. All-capital abbreviations are written without periods (YMCA, AFL-CIO, CN, MP, URL, RIP,) unless the abbreviation is geographical (U.S., B.C., P.E.I., T.O., U.K.) refers to a person (J.R. Ewing) or is a single letter (N. for north but NNW).

2. Most lowercase and mixed abbreviations take periods: f.o.b., Jr., Ont., No., B.Comm.

3. Mixed abbreviations that begin and end with a capital letter do not take periods: PhD, PoW, U of T.

4. Acronyms — abbreviations pronounced as words — formed from only the first letter of each principal word are all capitals: AIDS (acquired immune deficiency syndrome), NATO (North Atlantic Treaty Organization), NOW (National Organization for Women).

5. In most cases, acronyms formed from initial and other letters are upper and lowercase: Dofasco (Dominion Foundries and Steel Corp.), Nabisco (National Biscuit Co.), Norad (North American Aerospace Defence Command). Some exceptions have crept into common use (BMO, for Bank of Montreal); check individual listings.

6. Acronyms that have become common words are not capitalized: laser (light amplification by stimulated emission of radiation), radar (radio detection and ranging).

7. Metric symbols are not abbreviations and do not take periods: m, l, kW.

8. Plurals are MPs and PoWs; possessives MPs' and PoWs'.

Abbreviations

9. Most abbreviations are written without spaces: U.K., W.Va., P.Eng. But those written without periods are spaced: U of T.

10. Ampersands are allowed if used as part of a corporate name: A&W, Standard & Poor's, and in expressions like R&B. Usually, these are written without spaces when all-capital abbreviations are used and with spaces when they are not. Check individual listings.

See also the Canadian Press Stylebook, chapter Abbreviations and acronyms.

Compounds, Hyphens

1. Compound words may be written solid (website), open (oil rig) or hyphenated (yo-yo). Style is usually determined by the most common usage. A new compound is normally written at first as two or more words, becomes increasingly hyphenated and finally is combined into one word.

2. For compound words, follow the *Canadian Oxford Dictionary* unless the listing in this book differs. If the word is not listed in either, write it as separate words.

3. For compound modifiers, in general hyphenate when preceding a noun, but not if the meaning is instantly clear because of common usage of the term: three-under-par 69 *but* sales tax increase.

4. Hyphens are seldom needed with proper nouns (a North American trend), established foreign terms (a 10 per cent increase) or established compound nouns (a high school teacher).

5. Certain word combinations are often hyphenated even when standing alone: noun plus adjective (fire-resistant); noun plus participle (blood-stained); adjective plus participle (hard-earned); adjective plus noun (red-faced).

6. Hyphenate most well-known compounds of three words: happy-go-lucky; three-year-old. But there are exceptions: coat of arms; next of kin; no man's land.

7. Use a hyphen to avoid doubling a vowel, tripling a consonant or duplicating a prefix: co-operate; doll-like; sub-subcommittee.

8. Use a hyphen to join prefixes to proper names: anti-Liberal; pro-American.

9. Use a hyphen to join an initial capital with a word: T-shirt; S-bend.

Compounds, Hyphens

10. Use a hyphen to avoid awkward combinations of letters and to differentiate words: correspondent (letter writer) *but* co-respondent (in court); resign (quit) *but* re-sign (sign again).

11. Use a hyphen for the minus sign in temperatures and in bracketed political affiliations: -10 degrees; Donna Hooper (Con-Ont.)

For more information on compound words and hyphens, see the Canadian Press Stylebook, chapters Compound Words and Punctuation.

Place Names

1. National Geographic Society spellings are Canadian Press style for place names outside Canada with exceptions listed in the *Canadian Press Stylebook* and this guide.

2. The style authority for Canadian place names is the *Canadian Oxford Dictionary*, with some exceptions listed in this guide. If the place name is not in *Oxford*, consult the Geographical Names Board of Canada (http://www.nrcan.gc.ca/earth-sciences/geography/place-names/10786). For French place names, see next page.

French Capitalization

1. For the French names of organizations and the titles of books, songs, plays, movies, paintings and the like, The Canadian Press prefers the English form for the sake of readability: Quebec Liquor Corp., not Société des alcools du Québec; Remembrance of Things Past, not A la recherche du temps perdu.

2. In general, when the French name or title is used (in a quotation, for example) it should be followed by a description in English or a translation: Office de la langue française, or the government language agency; Le Malade imaginaire (The Imaginary Invalid).

3. If a work, organization or the like is commonly known by its French name, it need not be followed by a translation: La Bohème, Notre Dame, Le Droit.

4. The names of some organizations cannot really be translated (Conseil du patronat, the largest employer group in Quebec), or have become familiar in their French version (the Ecole polytechnique, the engineering school), or have no official English version (the Centrale des syndicats du Québec, the union that represents teachers).

5. The Canadian Press uses hyphens in multi-word French place names in Quebec and abroad: Trois-Rivières, Ste-Anne-de-Beaupré, Stanstead-Est, Ver-sur-Mer. Hyphens are omitted from purely English place names: Stanstead Plain, and if the first word is not a place name but a natural feature: Lac Barrière, Baie des Chaleurs.

6. For the names of saints (except in place names) use St. (not Ste.) for female as well as male: St. Dorothee.

French Capitalization

7. French dictionaries used by The Canadian Press are *Le Petit Robert* and *Le Petit Larousse*.

8. For the names of organizations, the first word is capitalized unless it is an article; other words except proper nouns are lowercase: (le) Service de perception, Emballages St-Laurent ltée.

9. For the titles of books, songs and the like, the first word is capitalized — the second too when the first is an article — and proper nouns: De la terre à la lune, Sur le pont d'Avignon, Les Liaisons dangereuses.

10. For the names of newspapers, the definite article, the first noun and proper nouns are capitalized: Le Journal de Montréal, Le Courrier du peuple.

A

A, An—Use "a" before consonant sounds: a historic building, a university, a one-way ticket, a euphemism, a 1914 novel. Use "an" before vowel sounds: an apple, an honest man, an S-bend, an 1814 novel, an RRSP.

A&E (specialty TV channel)

A&W

Abbott, Sir John (prime minister, 1891-92)

ABC (acceptable in all references for American Broadcasting Cos. — note plural)

Abella, Rosalie (Supreme Court of Canada justice)

abhor, abhorrence, abhorrent

Abidjan

Abitibi-Consolidated Inc. (TSX:A)

able seaman (*no abbvn.*)

Ablonczy, Diane (politician)

abominable snowman (yeti)

aboriginal (*adj., n. when referring to individual*); in Australia: Aboriginal or Aborigine

Aboriginal Peoples (all of Canada's Indians, Inuit and Métis)

abscess

abysmal (*not* -ss-)

abyss

Academy of Motion Picture Arts and Sciences, the academy

Acadie nouvelle, L' (newspaper in Caraquet, N.B.)

accessible (*not* -able)

accommodate (-mm-), accommodation

acetaminophen

acetylene

acetylsalicylic acid (ASA)

Achilles heel, tendon

acknowledgment

acquit, acquitted, acquittal

Act—Capitalize titles of parliamentary acts but not
subsequent references when the full name
is not used. And references to acts and bills
before royal assent are lowercase.
　　—Food and Drugs Act
　　—the food act says ...
　　—a proposed food act
acting, acting mayor James Borden, acting Sgt. Jane
Bloom
Action démocratique du Québec (ADQ or Action
démocratique *on second reference*)
actor (OK for both men and women)
ACTRA (Alliance of Canadian Cinema, Television
and Radio Artists)
Act 3, Scene 2; the third act, second scene
AD—Acceptable in all references for anno Domini
(in the year of the Lord). The abbreviation
goes before the figure for the year: AD 410. It
may also be used to refer to a century: the first
century AD.
adaptability
addendum, addenda
Addresses—Capitalize Street, Road, etc., used
with names; *but* King and Victoria streets.
Abbreviate in addresses when the number is
used; *but* 10 Downing Street, 24 Sussex Drive
(official residences).
　　—36 King St. E., Toronto M5C 2L9
　　—the Portage Avenue bus
　　—Wellington Crescent
　　—Cres., Blvd., Rd., Sq.
Adidas (*not* adidas)
adieu, adieus
adjuster (*not* -or)
administration, U.S. administration

Admiral John Smith (*no abbvn.*)
 —the admiral said ...
admiralty
 —the admiralty reported ...
 —first lord of the admiralty
 —the first lord's statement
 —Admiralty Court
admissible (*not* -able), admissibility
ad nauseam (*not* -eum)
Adonai
adrenalin
Adventist, Seventh-day
adverse (unfavourable), averse (reluctant)
advertise (*not* -ize)
adviser (*not* -or)
aerial
aerodynamics
Aeroflot airline
Aeronautics Act
aesthetic — *Use* esthetic
affect (*v.,* have effect on)
affidavit
affront (deliberate insult), effrontery (shameless
 insolence)
Afghan (*n.* and *adj., prefer to* Afghani)
aficionado (*one f*), aficionados
AFL-CIO (acceptable in all references for American
 Federation of Labor-Congress of Industrial
 Organizations)
African-American
African Union (AU, *but avoid*)
Afrikaans (language)
Afrikaner (person)
Afrocentric (*not* Africentric)
Aga Khan, the
Agence France-Presse (AFP)

agenda, agendas

agent provocateur, agents provocateurs

aggression, aggressive

aging (*not* ageing)

Aglukark, Susan

Aglukkaq, Leona (politician)

agreement
>—a Canada-U.S. agreement on power
>—General Agreement on Tariffs and Trade
>(GATT)

aide-de-camp, aides-de-camp

AIDS (for acquired immune deficiency syndrome)

airbag

airbase

Airbus

Air Canada (*no abbvn.*)
>—ACE Aviation Holdings Inc. (parent
>company; TSX:ACE.B)

Air Commodore John Smith (*no abbvn.*)
>—the air commodore said ...

Aircraft Names — Use a hyphen between symbols
>for the make or type and the model number.
>—DC-8L, B-57, A-320, MiG-25, CF-18
>—Yak-42, AN-154, IL-62, TU-144
>—*but* Dash 8 (*no hyphen*)

aircrew (*one word*)

airdrop (*one word*)

airfield (*one word*), Kandahar Airfield (*capped when
>part of official name*)

Air Force—Capitalize air force in references to
>the Royal Canadian Air Force both before
>unification in 1968 and after name change
>in August 2011. For other forces, lowercase
>air force when preceded by the name of the
>country.
>—British air force

—Royal Air Force
—U.S. or American air force
—U.S. 8th Air Force
—the air force planes
—Bomber Command
—Fleet Air Arm
—126 Squadron
—the squadron headquarters are ...

Air Force 1
Air India (*no hyphen*)
airlift (*n.* and *v.*)
Air Line Pilots Association (ALPA)
airmail (*n.* and *v.*)
airman (*no abbvn.*)
Air Marshal Lois Jones (*no abbvn.*)
—the air marshal said ...
Air Miles (loyalty program)
Airport—Lowercase unless the official name is
used.
—Pearson International Airport
—Toronto international airport
—Vancouver International Airport
—the Vancouver airport
airstrike *(one word)*
Air Vice-Marshal John Candy (*no abbvn.*)
—the air vice-marshal
a.k.a.
Aklavik, N.W.T.
Akwesasne Mohawk Territory
Al—In Arabic names of individuals, the articles el
and al may be used or dropped depending
on the person's preference or established
usage: Ayman al-Zawahri, al-Zawahri (*second
reference*); *but* Moammar Gadhafi, Gadhafi.
For other names, the article is usually uppercase:
Al Jazeera (Arab all-news channel)

Alabama (Ala.)

Alaska (*no abbvn.*)

Alberta (Alta.)

Alberta Heritage Savings Trust Fund (*no abbvn.*)

Alcoholics Anonymous (AA)

— Al-Anon (for relatives of alcoholics)

— Alateen (for children of alcoholics)

alderman, alderwoman (Ald.)

— Ald. John Doe

— alderwomen Jill Jones and Julia Wong

Alderwoods Group Inc.

— formerly Loewen Group Inc.

Alghabra, Omar (politician)

Algonquian (aboriginal language family)

Algonquin (Ojibwa dialect)

Al Jazeera (Arab all-news channel)

Allah

Allahu akbar! (God is great)

all-America (team), all-American (individual)

Allan Cup (hockey)

Alliance of Canadian Cinema, Television and Radio Artists (ACTRA)

Allied forces, the Allies (in world wars)

allophone (*but avoid*)

allot, allotted, allotting

all ready (set to go), already (beforehand)

all right (*two words; not* alright)

All Saints' Day (Nov. 1)

all-star

— an all-star team, game

— The Canadian Press's all-star selections

— National League All-Stars (team)

allusion (indirect reference), illusion (false impression)

Almighty, the

Alouette 1, 2 (satellites)

Alps, *but* alpine skiing

al-Qaida

already (beforehand)

al-Shabab (Somali militant group)

alternate (one after the other), alternative (one or the other)

aluminum

alumna, alumnae (*fem.*)

alumnus, alumni

Alzheimer's disease (*but* Alzheimer Society of Canada)

a.m., p.m. (*lowercase*)
—2 p.m., 2:30 a.m. EST, EDT

a mari usque ad mare (from sea to sea)

ambassador, the U.S. ambassador
—Ambassador Michael Wilson (capitalize before a name)

Amber Alert (child-abduction response system)

ambience

Ambrozic, Aloysius (1930-2011, Roman Catholic cardinal and archbishop of Toronto)

amendment, Fifth Amendment (U.S.)

American Federation of Labor-Congress of Industrial Organizations (AFL-CIO)

American Indian Movement (AIM)

American Telephone and Telegraph Co. (AT&T)

America's Cup (yachting)

amiable (of people), amicable (of things)

amok (*not* amuck)

Ampersand — Use when part of an official name: H&R Block and in expressions such as B&B (bed and breakfast). Write out in other uses: Ian and Sylvia.

Amtrak (*not* Amtrack)

analogous

analysis, analyses

analyze (*not* -se), analyzing

anemia, anemic

anesthesia, anesthetic, anesthetist

aneurysm

Anglican Church of Canada
>   —Anglican communion
>   —Anglican Church Women
>   —High Church, Low Church

Anglo, Anglo-Quebecer, Anglos

anglophone (*lowercase*)

Anik F1, F2 (satellites)

Animals—Capitalize breed names derived from proper names except where usage has established the lowercase.
>   —Holstein-Friesian *but* shorthorn
>   —Clydesdale *but* palomino
>   —Newfoundland dog *but* dachshund
>   —Siamese cat *but* angora

anoint

anomaly, anomalies

anorexia nervosa, anorexic

ante (prefix), antechamber, antedate, antenatal, anteroom

antenna, antennae (*pl.* for feelers of insect, etc.), antennas (*pl.* for aerials)

anti- (*prefix*), anti-aircraft, anti-Communist, antihistamine, anti-intellectual, anti-Semitic, antitrust, antivirus, antiwar

antivenin (*not* anti-venom)

anybody

anyhow

anymore (any longer)

any more (*as in* "I don't want any more candy")

anyone

anyplace

anything

any time (*two words*)
anyway
AOL Canada Inc.
apartheid
Apartment—Capitalize when used specifically, as when followed by a number; abbreviate when used in numbered addresses.
—the Rockingham Apartments
—in Apt. 207
—Apt. 207, Midtown Terrace
APEC (Asia-Pacific Economic Cooperation)
apostle, Twelve Apostles
—the Apostle Paul
—Paul the Apostle
app (short for computer application)
— mobile app, iPad app
appal, appalled, appalling
Appaloosa
apparatus, apparatuses
appeal, appealed, appealing, appealingly
Appeal Court
appellant
appellate division (of Supreme Court)
appendix, appendixes
Apples—Capitalize varieties.
—McIntosh, Golden Delicious, Ida Red
April (*no abbvn.*)
April Fools' Day (April 1)
Aqaba, Gulf of
Aqua-Lung (trademark for an underwater breathing device)
aquarium, aquariums
Arabian Gulf
— *Use* Persian Gulf
arabic numerals
Arafat, Yasser (PLO, 1929-2004)

Aransas (*not* Arkansas) refuge

arbour

arc, arcing, arced

Arcand, Denys (movies)

ArcelorMittal Canada (subsidiary of ArcelorMittal SA; formerly Mittal Canada Inc.)

Archbishop—Capitalize before a name and when the full title is used.

　—Archbishop John Smith

　—Archbishop of York

　—the archbishop said ...

archdiocese, Toronto archdiocese

archeological, archeologist, archeology

Arctic—Capitalize when referring to the Arctic region: Arctic Circle, Arctic Ocean, Arctic char, Arctic fox, Arctic plant. Lowercase when meaning very cold: arctic chill, arctic temperatures.

Arden, Jann (musician)

ardour

Argentine (*not* Argentinian)

argyle socks, sweater

Argyll and Sutherland Highlanders of Canada

Arizona (Ariz.)

Arkansas (Ark.) *but* Aransas refuge (for wildlife)

Armed Forces, the Forces (capped for Canada only)

armful, armfuls

armour

arm's-length *(adj.)*

Army—Capitalize Canadian Army when referring to force both pre-unification in 1968 and after name change in August 2011. For other forces, lowercase army when preceded by the name of the country.

　—Canadian Army until 1968 and after August 2011

A

—British army
—British 21st Army
—a convoy of army vehicles
—1st Canadian Division
—3rd Infantry Brigade
—Royal 22e Regiment
—B Company

Art—Lowercase art styles, schools, movements, etc.,
unless the word is derived from a proper noun
or can be confused with a common word.
—art deco, art nouveau
—baroque
—cubism, cubist
—Dada, Dadaism
—Gothic
—impressionism, impressionist
—neoclassical
—Renaissance
—Romanesque

arteriosclerosis
Arthabaska, Que. (Athabasca, Alta.)
arthroscopy
article
—a paragraph of Article 4
—Art. 4, Sec. 1, reads:
artifact
Arviat, Nunavut (formerly Eskimo Point)
Aryan Nations (white supremacist group)
ascend, ascendance, ascendant, ascension, ascent
—Ascension Day
Ashrawi, Hanan (Palestinian)
Ashton, Niki (MP)
Ash Wednesday
asinine
asphalt
Aspirin (trademark in Canada)

Assad, Bashar (Syria)

assassin, assassination

assembly

—National Assembly (national legislative body)

—Quebec national assembly (provincial body)

—legislative assembly

assistant (*lowercase*), assistant attorney general Erin Keenan

assisted suicide, assisted death

assizes, spring assizes

Associated Press, The (for AP)

—and The Associated Press said ...

—the Associated Press story said ...

—the AP (*second reference; lowercase* the)

Association of South East Asian Nations (ASEAN)

Associations—Capitalize names, but follow French style for French names.

—Société pour vaincre la pollution

—Association of the Scientific, Engineering and Technological Community of Canada (Scitec)

—Canadian Bankers Association

—the association meeting

Astronomy—Capitalize the proper names of planets, stars, constellations; capitalize only the proper-noun element of the name of comets, etc.; lowercase sun and moon. In general, lowercase earth, but capitalize it when referred to as an astronomical body.

—Saturn, North Star, Orion

—Halley's comet, Crab nebula

—down to earth

—heaven on earth

—The planets closest to the sun are Mercury, Venus and Earth.

—The astronauts turned back to Earth.

Astroturf (trademark for artificial grass or turf)

Atamanenko, Alex (politician)

AT&T (*no spaces*), for American Telephone and
Telegraph Co.

Athabasca, Alta. (Arthabaska, Que.)

Athapaskan (aboriginal languages)

atherosclerosis (a form of arteriosclerosis with fatty
degeneration)

Athlete of the Year

Athletes Can (*not* CAN)

athlete's foot

Atikamekw (First Nations in Quebec)

Atlantic provinces (N.B., N.L., N.S., P.E.I.)

Atomic Energy of Canada Ltd. (AECL *OK in second
reference*)

attorney (U.S.; *prefer* lawyer)

attorney, Crown
        —Crown attorney Ellen Tomcik
        —power of attorney (*no hyphens*)

attorney general, attorneys general
        —Attorney General Madalene Phillips

Audit Bureau of Circulations (ABC)

auditor general, auditors general, auditor general
        Michael Ferguson *(lowercase)*

auger (tool for boring holes)

augur (bode)

Augustyn, Frank (ballet)

Aulavik National Park (Banks Island)

aurora borealis (northern lights); aurora australis
        (southern equivalent)
        —Aurora (patrol aircraft)

authority
        —St. Lawrence Seaway Authority

authorize

automaker, autoworker (*but* Canadian Auto Workers
        union)

automated banking machine, ABM (*avoid* ABM
machine *as redundant*)
— *also ATM (automated teller machine)*
automaton, automatons
auto pact (signed January 1965)
Auyuittuq National Park (Baffin Island)
avant-garde
Avenue—Capitalize when used with names;
abbreviate in numbered street addresses.
—along Portage Avenue
—the Portage Avenue bus
—506 Curry Ave., Windsor, Ont. N9B 2B9
averse (reluctant), adverse (unfavourable)
avocado, avocados
Avro Arrow (the CF-105 interceptor aircraft built by
A.V. Roe Canada Ltd. in the 1950s)
AWACS (for airborne warning and control system)
Awards—Capitalize specific awards.
—National Newspaper Awards (NNA)
—the awards were presented ...
—Governor General's Awards
—Nobel Peace Prize
—Nobel Prize in chemistry
—Nobel Prize winner
—Pulitzer Prize
—Pulitzer Prize-winning author
—Academy Awards
awhile *(adv.), but* a while *(n.)*
AWL (*not* AWOL)
— absent without leave; *but avoid*
axe (*not* ax), axing
Axel (figure-skating jump)
axis, axes
—Axis, the (Second World War alliance of
Germany, Italy and Japan)

A

Aykroyd, Dan (comic)
Azerbaijan
AZT (HIV-AIDS drug, often called zidovudine)

B

Baath party (Iraq), Baathist (party member)
baby boom, baby boomer, baby boom generation
babysit, babysitter
baccalaureate
Bachand, Claude (politician)
bachelor
>—bachelor of arts (BA), a bachelor's degree
>—bachelor of laws (LLB, *but avoid)*
>—bachelor of science (B.Sc.)
>—honours bachelor degree
bacillus, bacilli
backbench members, backbenchers, backbenches
backbone, back burner, backlog, back roads,
>backstage, backstop (*n.* and *v.*), backup (*n.*
>and *adj.),* backyard
bacterium, bacteria
Baha'i (*n.* and *adj.*)
>—two Baha'is
>—the Baha'i faith
Bahamas, the
Bahamian (*not* Bahaman)
Bahrain
bail (water or bond)
bail out (of plane)
baked alaska
balaclava
bale (hay)
balk
balkanize
ball, ball club, ball game *but* ballplayer, ballpark
balloon, ballooning, balloonist
ballot, balloting
ballpoint
ballroom, Crystal Ballroom
baloney (slang — nonsense; also informal —
>bologna sausage)

B

band, the God's River band
Band-Aid (trademark for an adhesive bandage)
B&B (*no spaces*), bed and breakfast
banister (*not* -nn-)
banjo, banjos
Banks—Short forms, rather than corporate names,
may be used on first reference when their use
is widespread. *See also separate bank listings.*
   —BMO (Bank of Montreal)
   —CIBC (Canadian Imperial Bank of
Commerce)
   —HSBC (HSBC Bank Canada)
   —RBC, Royal Bank (Royal Bank of Canada)
   —Scotiabank (Bank of Nova Scotia)
   —TD Bank (Toronto-Dominion Bank)
   —Bank of Canada
   —World Bank
   —the bank's lending policy
baptize (*not* -s-)
bar
   —Canadian Bar Association (CBA, *but avoid)*
   —Bar of the Province of Quebec
(organization)
   —*but* Quebec bar, Montreal bar, called to the
bar
Barbados (one island; *do not use* the Barbados)
barbecue (*not* -que), barbecuing
barbiturate
Bardot, Brigitte
barefoot (*no hyphen*)
bar mitzvah (for boy marking 13th birthday), bat
mitzvah (for girl)
Barnard, Dr. Christiaan (1922-2001)
baroque
Barren Lands, the Barrens
Barrick Gold Inc. (TSX:ABX)

Barron's (financial weekly published by Dow Jones)

Baryshnikov, Mikhail (ballet)

Baseball—at bat (*but* five at-bats), backstop, ball club, ballpark, ballplayer, baseline, bullpen, centre field, centre-fielder, centre-field fence, change-up, double-A, doubleheader, double-play, earned-run average, fastball, first baseman, home plate, home run, left-fielder, left-hander, line up (*v.*), lineup (*n.*), major league (*n.*), major-league (*adj.*), a major-leaguer (*n.*), pinch hit (*n.* and *v.*), pinch-hitter (*n.*), play off (*v.*), playoff (*n., adj.*), RBI(s), put out (*v.*), putout (*n.*), right-fielder, right-hander, shortstop, shut out (*v.*), shutout (*n., adj.*), single-A, split-finger fastball, triple-A, triple-play, twi-night doubleheader

Basel, Switzerland

BASIC (for beginner's all-purpose symbolic instruction code)

basis, bases

Basketball—backboard, backcourt, baseline, field goal, foul line, foul shot, free throw, free-throw line, frontcourt, full-court press, goaltending, half-court pass, halftime, in-bounds pass, jump ball, jump shot, layup, man-to-man (*adj.*), midcourt, play off (*v.*), playoff (*n., adj.*), three-point play, three-pointer

basset (dog)

battalion, 3rd Battalion

Battle Harbour, N.L.

battle royal

Battles—Capitalize specific ones.
　　　—Battle of the Plains of Abraham
　　　—Battle of Britain

bauxite

B

bay, Hudson Bay, Bay of Quinte
    —Hudson's Bay Co., the Bay
bazaar
BB (shot)
BC—Acceptable in all references for before Christ. It follows the year or the century: 55 BC, the second century BC.
BCE Inc. (TSX:BCE)
        —Bell Canada
        —Bell Aliant (TSX:BA.UN)
        —Bell ExpressVu
        —Bell Mobility
        —Sympatico (Internet service)
BC Ferries *(no periods)*
BC Hydro *(no periods)*
beau, beaus
beef Stroganoff
Beethoven, Ludwig van (*not* von) (1770-1827)
behaviour
behoove (*not* behove)
Beijing (formerly Peking)
Belarus (formerly Byelorussia), Belarusian
Belize (formerly British Honduras)
belligerent
Bell Media (formerly CTVglobemedia)
bellwether
Belmont Stakes
beluga (whale)
benefit, benefited, benefiting
Benin (Dahomey until 1975)
Bergen, Candice (MP)
Bergeron, Stéphane (politician)
Berkeley, Calif.
Berlin Wall
Bermudian (*not* Bermudan)
Bern, Switzerland
berserk

Berton, Pierre (1920-2004)

besieged (*not* beseiged)

bestseller (*one word),* bestselling author

bettor (one who wagers)

Beverly Hills, Calif.

Bevilacqua, Maurizio (politician)

BHP Billiton Ltd. (Australia-based mining company)

Bible, Bible Belt

    —*but* the fisherman's bible

biblical

Bic (trademark for pen)

bicultural, bilingual (*no hyphen*)

Biennial, bimonthly, biweekly—These terms are ambiguous and can mean two different things. *Prefer* every two years, twice a month, twice a week, etc.

Big Ten (universities)

big-time (*adj.*), big time (*n.*)

bill

    —Bill 101

    —a proposed bill of rights

billet, billeted, billeting

Binghamton, N.Y.

bin Laden, Osama

bioterrorism, bioterrorist

biracial (*no hyphen*)

birdie (one stroke under par in golf)

Birks Jewellers (store)

    —Henry Birks and Sons Inc.

Birney, Earle (poet, 1904-1995)

birth, birthday, birthmark, birthrate, birthright

Bishkek, Kyrgyzstan (formerly Frunze, Kirghizia)

Bishop—Capitalize before a name and when the full title is used.

    —Bishop Edward Tremaine

    —Bishop of London

—the bishop's letter

Bismarck (*not* -rk)

bismuth (element)

Bitcoin (virtual currency concept); *but* 75 bitcoins (lowercase)

bitumen (the unrefined, thickest form of petroleum, extracted from oilsands)

— diluted bitumen (*or* dilbit, *but avoid*)

black (*lowercase* for race)

BlackBerry (wireless device maker, formerly Research in Motion Inc.) (TSX:BB); BlackBerrys

blackfly, blackflies

Blackhawks, Chicago

Black Muslim (member of Black Muslims organization; official name: the Nation of Islam)

black out (*v.*), blackout (*n.* and *adj.*)

Black Panther (member of Black Panthers organization)

Blaney, Steven (MP)

bleached-kraft pulp

blindsided

bloc (of parties, countries; voted as a bloc)

—Bloc Québécois

—former East Bloc

block (of shares, seats; also mental block)

blog, blogger, blogging

blond (*n.* and *adj.* for all uses; do not use blonde)

bloodbath *(one word)*

bloodthirsty *(one word)*

Bloody Mary (nickname for Mary I), bloody mary (cocktail)

blue, Double Blue (Toronto Argonauts)

blue line (hockey)

Bluenose II (ship)

Blu-ray (*lowercase* r)

BMO Financial Group (TSX:BMO)
> —BMO Bank of Montreal (Canadian banking operation)

B'nai Brith (Sons of the Covenant)

BNN—Use Business News Network *in first reference* (formerly Report on Business Television)

Board—Uppercase when using the formal name of a board. Otherwise, lowercase.
> —Toronto District School Board, but Toronto school board, public school board
> —Board of Trade, the board
> —Canadian Wheat Board, the wheat board
> —Treasury Board, the board

boat, lifeboat, motorboat, powerboat, sailboat

bobblehead

bobsled, bobsledding
> —Bobsleigh Canada

bocce (game)

bodycheck

bodyguard (*no hyphen*)

boe per day (*prefer* barrels of oil equivalent per day*)*

bogey, bogeys, bogeyed (for one over par)

bohemian (unconventional); Bohemian (of Czech region)

boldface (type)

Bomarc-A, Bomarc-B

bombardier (*no abbvn.*)

Bombardier Inc. (TSX:BBD.B)

Bombay — *Use* Mumbai

bombshell (*one word*)

bona fide (*adj.* — genuine; *adv.* — genuinely), bona fides (*n.* — proof of status)

bonspiel

bonus, bonuses

bookkeeper, bookkeeping

Book of Common Prayer

B

Book of Revelation (*not* Revelations)
Bophuthatswana (former homeland state in South
      Africa)
borscht, Borscht Belt
Bosnia-Herzegovina, Bosnia
Botox (trademark)
Bouctouche, N.B.
Boulevard—Capitalize when used with names;
      abbreviate in numbered street addresses.
      —on Decarie Boulevard
      —123 Decarie Blvd.
bound (*suffix*), eastbound, northbound, stormbound
bourbon (American whiskey)
Bourgeoys, St. Marguerite (Canada's first woman
      saint, 1620-1700)
Boutros-Ghali, Boutros
bovine spongiform encephalopathy (better known
      as mad cow disease; BSE OK *but explain*)
bowl, Rose Bowl, Super Bowl
bowling
      —fivepin, tenpin
boxcar
Boxing—Most weight classes are one word:
      flyweight, bantamweight, heavyweight.
      —knockout
boyfriend, girlfriend
braggadocio
braille
Brantford Expositor
Brasilia (capital of Brazil)
Bravo (*not* Bravo!) TV channel
breach (*n.* — breaking or neglect; *v.* — break
      through)
break (*v.*), break away, break down, break even,
      break in, break off, break out, break up

break (*n.*), breakaway, breakdance, breakdown,
    break-in, breakneck, breakout, breakup,
    breakthrough, breakwater
breastfeed
breathalyzer
Brébeuf, St. Jean de (1593-1649)
breech (back part of gun barrel), breeches (short
    trousers), breeches-buoy
Breitkreuz, Garry (politician)
Bren gun
Bre-X Minerals Ltd. (defunct)
Brezhnev, Leonid (1906-1982)
bridge, Lions Gate Bridge, Sydney Harbour Bridge
Bridle Path (upscale neighbourhood in Toronto; *not*
    Bridal Path)

Brier (curling tournament), Tim Hortons Brier
brigadier (Brig. Arthur Smith)
brigadier-general (Brig.-Gen. Arthur Smith)
Brink's Canada Ltd.
    —*but* a Brinks truck, Brinks guard (*no
    apostrophe*)
Britain—The one island: England, Scotland, Wales.
    (*But* British also covers Northern Ireland.)
Britannia
British Airways (*no abbvn.*)
British Columbia (B.C.)
British Commonwealth (*prefer* the Commonwealth)
British North America Act (BNA Act)
British thermal unit(s), BTU(s)
Briton (*not* Britisher)
broach (open; begin to talk about)
broccoli
Brockville Recorder and Times
Bromo Seltzer (trademark for bicarbonate of soda)
brooch (ornament)

B

Bros. for company names *but* Brothers with
    entertainment groups: the Mills Brothers
brouhaha
Brueggergosman, Measha (singer)
Bruinooge, Rod (politician)
brussels sprouts
Brzezinski, Zbigniew
Buckingham Palace
Buddha, Buddhism, Buddhist
budget, budgetary, budgeted, budgeting
buffalo, buffaloes *(prefer bison for North American*
    species)
Building—Capitalize important buildings.
    —Parliament Buildings
    —Empire State Building
    —Aetna Life building
build up (*v.*), buildup (*n., adj.*), built-up (*adj*)
Bujold, Geneviève (actor)
bulimia
bullmastiff *(one word)*
Bullock, Sandra (actor)
bull's-eye
bumf (papers, documents)
bungee jumping
Bunyan, Paul
buoy, buoyant, buoyancy
bureau, bureaus
burka
Burkina Faso (formerly Upper Volta)
Burk's Falls, Ont.
Burton, Richard (actor, 1925-1984)
bus (vehicle), buses, busing
Busan, South Korea (*not* Pusan)
Bush, George W. (use initial to distinguish from
    father, George Bush)
businessman, businesswoman

Business News Network (formerly Report on
     Business Television; BNN *on second reference*)
buss (kiss), busses
Buthelezi, Mangosuthu (Zulu leader)
buttonhole (*no hyphen*)
Buy American (protectionist provisions in U.S.
     job-creation measures)
byelection, bylaw, byline, bypass, byproduct (*no
     hyphen*)
byte (unit of computer memory)

C

C (use for Canadian currency: C$500)

cabinet, cabinet council

cable TV (*no hyphen*)

cacophony

cactus, cacti

cadet

    —officer cadet (*no abbvn.*)

    —Officer Cadet Garth Atkins

Cadillac

CAE Inc. (TSX:CAE)

Caesar, Julius (c. 102-44 BC)

caesarean birth, section (*lowercase*), *but* C-section

caesar salad

Caesars Palace (Las Vegas — *no apostrophe*)

café

caffeine

Cage, Nicolas (actor)

caisse populaire (credit union), caisses populaires

Calcutta (*avoid;* former name of Indian city of
    Kolkata)

Calder Memorial Trophy (NHL's top rookie)

calibre, a .45-calibre pistol

California (Calif.)

Callaghan, Morley (novelist, 1903-1990)

Callbeck, Catherine (senator)

callisthenics

callous (*adj.* — unfeeling), callus (*n.* — thickened
    skin)

call-up (*n.*)

calorie

camaraderie

Cambodia (Kampuchea 1975-90)

Canada

    —Central Canada (Ontario and Quebec)

    —Eastern Canada (the Atlantic provinces,
    Quebec and Ontario)

—Lower Canada (present-day Quebec)
—Upper Canada (present-day Ontario)
—Western Canada (Manitoba, Saskatchewan, Alberta and British Columbia)
Canada AM (CTV show)
Canada Border Services Agency, customs
    —go through customs, a customs officer
Canada Council for the Arts, Canada Council, the council
Canada Cup (hockey)
Canada Day (July 1)
Canada Industrial Relations Board (CIRB, *but avoid*)
Canada Mortgage and Housing Corp. (CMHC)
Canada NewsWire (CNW in second reference)
Canada Pension Plan (CPP, *but avoid*)
Canada Revenue Agency (formerly Canada Customs and Revenue Agency)
Canadarm 2
Canada Savings Bond (CSB)
Canada's Cup (yachting)
Canada West Foundation
Canada-wide (*adj.*)
Canadian Alliance (now Conservative Party of Canada)
Canadian Association of Broadcasters (CAB)
Canadian Auto Workers (CAW *in second reference*)
Canadian Bankers Association
Canadian Blood Services
Canadian Coast Guard
    —the coast guard ship
    —coastguardman (*one word*)
Canadian Community Newspapers Association
Canadian Conference of Catholic Bishops (*not* Council)
Canadian Food Inspection Agency

C

Canadian Forces, the Forces (*capped for Canadian only*)
　　—Canadian Forces Headquarters (CFHQ, *but avoid*)
　　—a Canadian Forces base
　　—Canadian Forces Base Trenton, CFB Trenton *(second reference)*
　　—CFB TRENTON (placeline)
Canadian government
Canadian Heritage (for Department of Canadian Heritage; *do not use* Heritage Canada, which is an unrelated organization)
Canadian Institutes of Health Research (formerly Medical Research Council of Canada)
Canadian Interuniversity Sport (CIS *in second reference*)
Canadian Journalism Fellowships (formerly Southam Fellowships)
　　—Canadian Journalism Fellow
Canadian Manufacturers & Exporters (formerly Alliance of Manufacturers & Exporters Canada)
Canadian National, or CN
　　—Canadian National Railway Co. (formal name; TSX:CNR)
　　—CN Tower
Canadian National Institute for the Blind — *Use* CNIB
Canadian Newspaper Association (CNA, *but avoid*)
Canadian Nuclear Safety Commission (formerly Atomic Energy Control Board)
Canadian Opera Company (*not* Co.)
Canadian Pacific Railway Ltd. (TSX:CP)
　　—Canadian Pacific or CP *on second reference*
Canadian Paediatric Society
Canadian Press, The
Canadian Professional Golfers' Association (CPGA)

Canadian Radio-television and Telecommunications
    Commission (CRTC *OK* in first reference)
Canadian Security Establishment (Canada's electronic
    spy agency; CSE, *but avoid; formerly* Canadian
    Security Establishment Canada)
Canadian Security Intelligence Service (CSIS)
Canadian Shield
Canadian Space Agency
Canadian Taxpayers Federation
Canadian Tire Corp. Ltd. (TSX:CTC.A)
Canadian Transportation Agency
Canadian Wheat Board (*no abbvn.*)
Canadian Wildlife Service (*no abbvn.*)
canal, Panama Canal, Suez Canal, Welland Canal
    —Panama Canal Zone (district)
cancel, cancelled, cancelling
Cancer, Tropic of
Cancon (*OK in second reference* for Canadian
    content)
candour
Candu (for Canadian deuterium uranium reactor)
Canfor Corp. (TSX:CFP)
canister
canoeist
cantaloupe
canto, cantos
Canuck
canvas, canvases (cloth, painting)
canvass (*v.* — examine; seek votes, orders; *n.* —
    process of canvassing)
canyon, Grand Canyon
cap-and-trade, cap-and-trade emissions (hyphens for
    n. and *adj.)*
Cap-aux-Meules, Que.
Cape Breton (*never in placeline*)
Cape Town (*two words*)

C

Capitol (building at Washington, D.C.) *but* state
     capitol (*lowercase*)
cappuccino, cappuccinos
captain, Capt. (*but* team captain Joan Verona)
Cara Operations Ltd.
carat (gems), karat (gold), caret (printing)
carburetor
cardinal (*no abbvn.*)
     —Cardinal John Smith
     —the cardinal (or Smith) said ...
CARE (for Co-operative for American Relief
     Everywhere Inc.)
caregiver
cargo, cargoes
Caribbean Community (federation)
Caribbean Free Trade Area (Carifta, *but avoid*)
Cariboo Mountains (B.C.)
caribou (deer), Caribou (Inuit, plane)
Caribou Mountains (Alta.)
carillon, carillonneur
carjack, carjacking (*v.* and *n.*)
Carleton, N.S. and Que.
     —Carleton Place, Ont.
     —Carleton University (Ottawa)
     —Carleton Village, N.S.
     —*but* Carlton, Sask.
     —Carlton Street (Toronto)
     —Ritz-Carlton Hotel
carmaker
carpet, carpet-bag, carpet-sweeper
Cartier, George-Etienne (1814-1873)
cartilage
cassette, videocassette
catalogue (*not* catalog)
catch-22 (a dilemma from which there is no escape);
     Catch-22 (Joseph Heller's book)

category, Category 2

Caterpillar, a Cat (trademark for a tractor)

catholic (universal)

Catholic, Catholicism (*but* specify Roman Catholic
or Roman Catholicism *on first reference* if
reference excludes Eastern-rites Catholic
churches.

CAT scan — *Use* CT scan

Cattle—Capitalize breed names derived from proper
names except where usage has established the
lowercase.

—Holstein-Friesian

—Jersey, Guernsey, Ayrshire

—shorthorn

Caucasian

cave in (*v.*), cave-in (*n.*)

CBC (*acceptable in all references* for Canadian
Broadcasting Corp.)

—CBC-TV, CBC Radio One, CBC Radio Two

—*The Current, The National, News Network*

CBS Inc.

—CBS's coverage

cease fire (*v.*), ceasefire (*n.*)

cease trade (*v.*), cease-trade order (*adj.*)

Ceausescu, Nicolae (Romanian leader, 1918-1989)

Celanese (trademark for acetate, nylon, polyester,
rayon)

Celestica Inc. (TSX:CLS)

cellblock (in jail)

cellophane, celluloid, cellulose

cellphone (cellular phone)

Celsius, -30 C (hyphen, no period; specify Celsius
only to avoid confusion)

cement (powder; used in concrete)

cemetery, Ocean View Cemetery

census, censuses, census day

C

Centennial Year, the Centennial (1967)
>—*but* Canada's centennial
>—centennial celebrations

Centers for Disease Control and Prevention (Atlanta, full name; Centers for Disease Control *OK in first reference)*
>—*Use* U.S. Centers for Disease Control *if necessary* to make clear it is American centre

centimetre (cm — *sing.* and *pl.* metric symbol, no period)

Central Canada (Ontario and Quebec)

Central Committee

Centrale de l'enseignement du Québec (Quebec teachers federation)

centre, centred, centring
>—centre on (*not* around)
>—centre field (baseball)
>—centre-fielder
>—centre-field wall
>—John F. Kennedy Center for the Performing Arts
>—Air Canada Centre
>—Rockefeller Center

Centre of Forensic Sciences (Toronto)

centurion (Roman soldier), Centurion (tank)

century, 20th century, second-century Rome

CEO (*OK in first reference* for chief executive officer)

CFCs (chlorofluorocarbons)

CF-18 (Canadian designation for the McDonnell Douglas aircraft)

chamber, lower chamber
>—Chamber of Deputies
>—Halifax Chamber of Commerce
>—the chamber of commerce

changeover (*n.*), change over (*v.*)

channel
>   —Channel 10 (television)
>   —English Channel and the Channel
>   —Channel Tunnel (between Britain and France)

chaperone (*not* -on)

Chappaquiddick Island, Mass.

chapter (*no abbvn.*), Chapter 1

chargé(s) d'affaires, chargé d'affaires John O'Hara

chargeback (*n.* and *adj.*)

charley horse

Charlottetown accord

Charter of Rights and Freedoms, the charter, charter rights

chat room

check (restaurant bill)

checkerboard, checkers, checkered flag (motor racing), checkered career

check off (*v.*), checkoff (*n.*)

checkpoint (*one word*), Checkpoint Charlie

check up (*v.*), checkup (*n.*)

Chedabucto Bay, N.S.

cheddar cheese

chef-d'oeuvre, chefs-d'oeuvre

Chekhov, Anton (Russian writer, 1860-1904)

Chemical elements—Write out *in first reference* (carbon dioxide) but symbols *OK in second reference* if popularly used: CO2.

Chennai, India (formerly Madras)

cheque (bank), chequebook

Chernomyrdin, Viktor (Russian politician)

cherub, cherubs

Chiang Kai-shek (1887-1975)

Chianti (wine)

chickenpox

chief

C

—Chief Tom Whitefeather
—police Chief Anna Myers
—fire Chief Ron Espy

chief master sergeant
—Chief Master Sgt. Phil McDonald

chief petty officer (*no abbvn.*)

chief warrant officer (*no abbvn.*)

childish (silly, puerile), childlike (innocent, trusting)

Children's Aid Society

Chile

chili, chilies
—chili con carne
—chili sauce

China, People's Republic of (mainland, *but prefer simply* China)

china (crockery)

Chinese (*n* and *adj.*)

Chinese Names—Use the official Chinese spelling, Pinyin, for most personal and place names: Hua Guofeng (formerly Hua Kuofeng). Note that the family name (Hua) normally precedes the given name (Guofeng). But westernized Chinese often follow English practice: Robert Chow (*not* Chow Robert).

Use the traditional spellings for Shanghai and Tibet. But use Zhou Enlai (*not* Chou En lai) and Mao Zedong (*not* Mao Tse-tung).

chinook

Chipewyan (aboriginal band)

chipmaker (*one word*)

chisel, chiselled, chiseller

chlorophyll

choose, chose, chosen, choosing, choosy

Chornobyl (Ukraine)

Choyce, Lesley (writer)

Chrétien, Jean

Christie's (auctioneer)

Christmas Day, Eve

chromosome

Church—Capitalize in names of religions and
buildings.

—Roman Catholic Church, Catholic Church,
Anglican Church; *but* the church (*lowercase*)

—St. Bartholomew's Church (building), the
church (building)

—a church building, church doctrine

Church of Christ, Scientist (Christian Science Church
OK in first reference)

Church of Jesus Christ of Latter-day Saints
(Mormons)

chute (sluice, slide, parachute)

chutzpah (gall, audacity)

CIBC (TSX:CM)

—CIBC (for Canadian Imperial Bank of
Commerce) *OK in first reference*

—CIBC World Markets Inc. (corporate and
investment banking arm); CIBC Wood Gundy
(retail investment division)

cigarette

cipher (*not* cypher)

circle (Circ.)

Circle, Arctic

—*but* arctic winds, temperatures

Cirque du soleil

cirrhosis

citizens band (CB, *but avoid*)

—citizens-band radio (*hyphen*)

city, city council

—Halifax City Hall (proper name)

—city hall (administration, building)

—City of Halifax (corp.)

—*but* in the city of Halifax

—Quebec City (Quebec in placelines)

C

City (television station in Toronto, Vancouver, Calgary, Edmonton and Winnipeg; formerly Citytv)

Civil Aeronautics Board (U.S.)

Civil Service Commission (*no abbvn.*)

civil war

　　—Spanish Civil War

　　—Civil War (U.S.)

clamour

clangour (*but* clangorous)

Claridge's (London hotel)

Clark, Joe (former prime minister)

Clarke, Austin (novelist)

Clarkson, Adrienne

Class—Lowercase school classes, except languages.

　　—class of '61

　　—mathematics class

　　—French class

class (military)

　　—S-class submarine

　　—tribal-class destroyer

class A, class B (shares)

clean up (*v.*), cleanup (*n.*)

clear cut (*v.*), clearcut (*n.*)

cliché

clientele

climactic (of a climax), climatic (of climate)

Clinton, Hillary Rodham

cloverleaf (on highways), cloverleafs

Club—Capitalize names.

　　—Rotary Club

　　—a club officer

CNIB (formerly Canadian National Institute for the Blind)

CN Tower (Toronto)

co- (prefix), coadjutor, co-author (*n. only*), coaxial,
co-chairman, coexist, co-host, co-operate,
co-ordinate, co-owner, co-pilot (*n. only*),
co-worker.

coast

—East Coast, West Coast, Gulf Coast (regions),
B.C. coast, Atlantic coast (shorelines)

coast guard

—Canadian Coast Guard

—U.S. Coast Guard

—the coast guard, the coast guard ship

coastline *(one word)*

cobalt-60

Cobol (common business oriented language)

Cobourg, Ont.

Coca-Cola, Coke (trademarks for cola drink)

coccus, cocci

cockney

code, city building code

—Criminal Code, the code

—Morse code

coed (*avoid* as a noun for female student. *OK* as an
adjective meaning coeducational: coed dorm)

Cogeco Cable Inc. (TSX:CCA)

cognoscente (*sing.*), cognoscenti (*pl.*)

coho (salmon — *sing.* and *pl.*)

Coke (as trade name for Coca-Cola)

Cold War

Colisée (Quebec City arena)

collectible(s)

College—Capitalize the names of universities and
colleges.

—McGill University

—University of Toronto (U of T)

—Victoria College

College of Cardinals

collegiate, York Collegiate (capitalize when part of
     official name)
Collins Bay, Ont.
     —Collins Bay Penitentiary
Colombia (South America)
Colombo Plan
colonel (Col. Eric Anderson)
Colorado (Colo.)
Colosseum (Rome)
colour, colourize, colourist *but* colorific
Colville, Alex (painter)
Comaneci, Nadia (former gymnast)
combat, combated, combatant
come back (*v.*), comeback (*n.*)
Come By Chance, N.L.
command, Maritime Command
commander (Cmdr. Wayne Elder)
     —lieutenant-commander (Lt.-Cmdr.)
     —wing commander (Wing Cmdr.)
commander-in-chief
commander of the Order of the British Empire (CBE)
commandment
     —the Ten Commandments
     —the Tenth Commandment
commando, commandos
command sergeant major
     —Command Sgt. Maj. Claude Laporte
commensurate
commiserate
Commission—Capitalize the proper name of
     government and royal commissions.
     —Commission on the Future of Health Care
     but the health-care commission
commissioner, information commissioner Suzanne
     Legault, privacy commissioner Daniel Therrien
     (lowercase)

commitment

committal

committed suicide (*avoid; prefer* 'died by suicide,'
'killed herself' *or* 'took his own life')

committee

—Commons finance committee

commodore (*no abbvn.*)

Common Prayer, Book of

Commons, House of

—the House, the Commons

common sense, a common-sense approach

commonwealth

—the Commonwealth

—Commonwealth of Australia

—Commonwealth Development Bank

—Commonwealth Games, the Games

—Co-operative Commonwealth Federation
(CCF)

communion, holy communion

—Anglican communion

communism (philosophical attitude)

Communist (party, government or member)

—anti-communist, non-communist,
pro-communist

communist ideals (philosophical)

Companies' Creditors Arrangement Act (CCAA *OK in
second reference*)

Company—Use Co. in business names.

—American Broadcasting Cos. (ABC)

—Brown Co.

—*but* Canadian Opera Company
(entertainment)

—B Company (military)

company quartermaster-sergeant (*no abbvn.*)

company sergeant major (Company Sgt. Maj. John
Jones)

—company sergeants major

compare to (liken to), compare with (check
    similarities and differences)
compatible
compel, compelled, compelling
competent (*not* -ant)
complementary (serving to complete),
    complimentary (expressing compliment; free)
concede
concept, conception
    —Immaculate Conception
concertgoer
concerto, concertos
Concorde (aircraft)
condole, condolence (*not* -ance)
Confederation (Canada)
    —Fathers of Confederation
Confederation of National Trade Unions (CNTU); in
    French, Confédération des syndicats nationaux
    (CSN)
conference
    —federal-provincial conference
    —Duke of Edinburgh's Study Conference
    —Law of the Sea conference
    —Conference Board of Canada
confidant (man), confidante (woman)
Confucian
Congo, Republic of (capital Brazzaville)
Congo (formerly Zaire, formal name Democratic
    Republic of Congo)
congregation
    —Congregation for the Doctrine of the Faith
    (Vatican)
Congress (U.S.)
    —*but* congressman, congressional
    —Sen. John Smith
    —Rep. Mary Smith
    —Congress party (India)

Congress of Racial Equality (CORE)

Connecticut (Conn.)

connoisseur (-nn-)

Connors, Stompin' Tom (singer-composer,
 1936-2013)

Conn Smythe Trophy (hockey)

conscientious

consensus (*not* consensus of opinion)

Conservative (party), conservative (political outlook)
 —Conservative Party of Canada (formal name)
 —small-c conservative

constable (Const.)
 —Const. Maria Huang
 —a city constable

constitution, the French Constitution, the
 constitution; *but* the Constitution (capped in
 all references to Canada)

consulate, French Consulate, the consulate

consul general, Consul General Guy Tremblay

consumer price index (CPI, *but avoid*)

Consumers' Association of Canada

consummate

contact (*v.*, *adj.* and *n.*)

Contadora (island near Panama)

Continent, the (Europe)

continental shelf

contralto, contraltos

controller (*no abbvn.*)
 —Controller Gillian Towers

convener (*not* -or)

converter (*not* -or)

cookbook

Cools, Anne (senator)

Coon Come, Matthew (Coon Come *in second
 reference)*

co-operate, co-operation

Co-operative Commonwealth Federation (CCF)

co-ordinate

copy editing, copy editor

copyright

  —Copyright, The Canadian Press

CORE (for Congress of Racial Equality)

co-respondent (divorce), correspondent (writer)

cornea (*sing.*), corneas (*pl.*)

Corner Brook, N.L.

Corner Brook Western Star

cornerstone, lay

Cornwall Standard-Freeholder

coronavirus (*one word*)

corporal (Cpl. Jane Smith)

  —lance-corporal (Lance-Cpl.)

Corporation—Use Corp. in business names.

  —British Broadcasting Corp. (BBC)

  —Canadian Broadcasting Corp. (*but* CBC preferred)

  —Ontario Lottery and Gaming Corp.

corral, corralled

Correctional Service Canada, correctional service

cosy (*not* cozy)

CO2 (OK *in second reference* for carbon dioxide)

council, city or county council, Peel regional council *but* Canada Council, Quebec Forest Industry Council, Council of Atlantic Premiers

councillor (Coun.)

  —Coun. Robert Jones

  —a city councillor

Council of Yukon First Nations

counsel, Crown counsel, Queen's counsel (QC, *but avoid*)

counsellor

counterattack, counter-intelligence, counter-proposal, counterterrorism countess

    —Sophie, Countess of Wessex (*not* Princess
    Sophie, Countess of Wessex), the countess

countrywide

County—Capitalize when preceding or following a
    specific term.

    —Huron County

    —County Derry

    —*but* in the county of Huron

coureur de bois, coureurs de bois

Court—Capitalize superior courts but not lower
    courts.

    —Admiralty Court

    —Appeal Court

    —Court of Queen's Bench

    —European Court of Justice

    —family court

    —Federal Court, Federal Appeal Court

    —judicial committee of the Privy Council

    —Ontario court of justice (lower court)

    —provincial court

    —small claims court

    —Superior Court (Que.)

    —Superior Court of Justice (Ontario)

    —Supreme Court (fed., prov., state)

    —Tax Court (Canada, U.S.)

    —territorial court (N.W.T.)

    —U.S. Court of Appeals

    —U.S. Court of Military Appeals

    —youth court

    —the court ordered

Courtenay, B.C.

courthouse, courtroom

court martial, courts martial (*n.*), court-martial (*v.*)

Court of St. James's

Covent Garden (*not* Gardens)

C

cover up (*v*.), coverup (*n*.)

crackpipe

craftman (*no abbvn.*)

    —Craftman Elwood Greene (military)

    —*but* craftsman (artisan)

Craigellachie, B.C. (where Last Spike was driven in railway in 1885)

Craigslist

creditor (one owed a debt; *not* -er)

Cree (*sing.* and *pl.*)

crescent (Cres.)

Crête, Paul (politician)

Creutzfeldt-Jakob disease (human spongiform encephalopathy; CJD OK *but explain*)

    —variant Creutzfeldt-Jakob disease (variant CJD; the form related to mad cow disease)

crewman, crewwoman, crew member

cricket

    —England-Australia Test match

    —the Test

    —the Ashes

Crime Stoppers (*two words*)

Criminal Code, the code

crisis, crises

criterion, criteria

criticism, criticize (*not* -ise)

Croat(s) (*n*.), Croatian (*adj*.)

CROP Inc. (Centre de recherches sur l'opinion publique; Quebec-based polling firm)

Crosby, Sidney (hockey)

cross-border

cross-checking

cross-country

cross-examine, cross-examination

crossfire

crossover (vehicle, music)

Crow, Sheryl (singer)

crowdsourcing, crowdfunding (*no hyphen*)

crown

> —the Crown (judge or prosecutor)
> —the Crown alleges ...
> —Crown attorney, counsel
> —Crown attorney Liz Baker
> —a Crown corporation, Crown land
> —a crown prince
> —*but* Crown Prince Rupert

Crowsnest Pass

Crucifixion

cruise (missile)

Crusades

crybaby (*no hyphen*), crybabies

CSeries jet (Bombardier)

CSI (TV show)

CT scan (computerized tomography)

CTVglobemedia (now Bell Media)

CTV News Channel

cubism, cubist

Cultural Revolution (China)

cummings, e.e. (1894-1962)

cup, Stanley Cup, the Cup (trophy)

> —America's Cup (yachting)
> —Canada Cup (hockey)
> —Canada's Cup (yachting)

cupful, cupfuls

Curia (Vatican office)

Curling—bonspiel, free-guard zone, hog line, in-turn draw, out-turn draw, shot rock

curriculum, curriculums

curtain, Iron Curtain

curtsy, curtsies

CUSO (OK *in first reference*, originally stood for Canadian University Service Overseas)

C

customs, Canada Border Services Agency
— a customs officer
— go through customs
CUV (crossover utility vehicle)
cyberattack, cyberbully, cybersecurity, cyberspace
(*but* U.S. Cyber Command)
cyclosporine
cystic fibrosis
czar, Czar Nicholas
Czech Republic

dachshund

Dacotah, Man.

Dacron (trademark for polyester fibre)

Dahomey (Benin since 1975)

Daimler AG

Dalai Lama, the

Dalmatian

dame, Dame Maggie Smith (*but avoid*), Smith (*second reference*)

damn, damned, damn it, God damn

Dances—Lowercase names.
>—breakdancing, bump, charleston, foxtrot, go-go, minuet, pas de deux, polka, polonaise, twist

danish (pastry)

Dar es Salaam
>—DAR ES SALAAM (in placelines)

Dari (language dominant in Afghanistan)

Dark Ages

Dash 8

data (*plural* in scientific writing but usually *singular* in other uses)

databank, database

dateline, placeline
>—*but* international date line

Dates—Write December 2004 without commas and Dec. 14, 2004, with commas. In dates, abbreviate the months except March, April, May, June and July: Aug. 1, May 3. Write Christmas 2005.
>—1997-98 but 1999-2002

Day—Capitalize religious holidays and feasts and all special times.
>—All Saints' Day
>—Christmas Eve
>—Earth Day
>—*but* election day

D

daycare (*n.*), daycare centre (*adj.*)

daylight (*not* daylight saving) time
> Applies from second Sunday in March until first Sunday in November except in regions that exempt themselves
> —ADT, EDT, etc.

daylong (*one word*)

day trader

D-Day (June 6, 1944)

DDT (dichlorodiphenyltrichloroethane)

de- (*prefix*), deactivate, debar, decompress, de-emphasize, de-escalate, defrost, de-ice, de-ink, deodorize, destabilize

de, der, di, du, d'—When lowercase in names, capitalize only at start of sentence.
> —de Gaulle, Charles
> —de Havilland Inc. (division of Bombardier Inc.)
> —De Laurentiis, Dino (movies)
> —deMille, Cecil B. (movies)
> —deWit, Willie (boxing)
> —de facto (two words — existing, whether legal or not)
> —de jure (two words — by right, by law; *but avoid*)
> —deluxe (*one word*)
> —de rigueur (*not* -geur)

dean, dean of arts

debacle

debonair

deceive, deceivable (*not* -eable), deceiver

decision-making

-decker, double-decker

Decorations—Capitalize specific names.
> —Distinguished Service Cross (DSC)

decrepit

D

deductible (*not* -able)

deejay — *Use* DJ

deepsea (*adj., no hyphen*)

Deep South (U.S.)

defence (*not* defense), *but* defensive

defenceman (*one word*)

defuse (remove fuse), diffuse (spread)

Dehcho First Nation, but Deh Cho for region of
     Northwest Territories

Deja View (specialty TV channel)

Delaware (Del.)

delicatessen

delta, Mekong River Delta

demagogue, demagogy (*not* -goguery)

demeanour

Democrat

Democratic party (U.S.)
     —New Democratic Party (NDP)
     —a New Democrat

Dene (pronounced Den'-neh)
     —Dene Nation (represents aboriginals in
     Northwest Territories)

Denendeh (Dene name for Northwest Territories)

Deng Xiaoping, Deng (1904-1997)

Denim Pine (trademark for wood stained blue by
     activities of mountain pine beetles)

Departments—Capitalize international, national
     and provincial government departments and
     ministries. Lowercase municipal, school and
     business departments.
     —Department of National Defence
     —Defence Department
     —Department of Indian and Northern Affairs
     —Indian Affairs Department
     —Vietnam Health Ministry

Lowercase department in plural uses.

—the Defence and Industry departments
Capitalize the proper-name element when standing alone and used as noun meaning the department.

—She went to Defence from Industry.

—*but* Toronto parks department

—McGill history department

It is not necessary to use the full formal name of a department if a shorter version is clear: Fisheries Department, *not* Department of Fisheries and Oceans or Fisheries and Oceans Canada.

dependant (*n.*), dependent (*adj.*), dependence (*not* -ance)

deprecate (disapprove), depreciate (belittle, lose value)

Depression (or Great Depression), the (1930s)

deputy

—Deputy Prime Minister Linda Graves, Deputy Chief Joe Jones (formal title)

—deputy premier Saul Hillier (informal position)

—deputy Speaker Jean Turcotte

—the deputy Speaker

—deputy Crown attorney Alys Yamata

de rigueur (*not* riguer)

descendant (offspring)

descendent (descending)

-designate, prime minister-designate John Block, the chairman-designate

desirable (*not* -eable)

desktop *(one word)*

desperate, desperation

despoliation (*not* despoilation)

detective

    —Det. Fred Lisak (police)

    —private detective James Brown

deterrent (*not* -ant)

Detroit Three (GM, Ford, Chrysler; *preferred to* Big Three except in historical references)

Deutsche Grammophon (recordings)

Deutschmark (*prefer* German mark)

developing nations (*not* Third World)

Devoir, Le (Montreal newspaper)

devotee

DEW (for Distant Early Warning) Line

Dhaka, Bangladesh

diabetes, Type 1, Type 2 diabetes

dialed, dialing

dial up *(v.)*, dial-up *(adj., n.)*

dialysis

diameter

Diana, or Princess of Wales (*not* Princess Diana)

diaphragm

diarrhea

Diavik (diamond mine in Northwest Territories)

DiCaprio, Leonardo (actor)

Dickensian

die, dying

Diefenbaker, John (1895-1979)

diehard

Diet (national legislative body)

dietitian

diffuse (spread), defuse (remove fuse)

Dijon mustard

dike (barrier; *not* dyke)

dilemma

dilettante, dilettantes

DiMaggio, Joe (1914-1999)

dining room

D

diocese, Hamilton diocese

Dion, Stéphane

diphtheria

diphthong

disaster, disastrous

disc, compact disc (CD), slipped disc, disc brake,
     disc jockey *but* floppy disk, diskette

discernible (*not* -able)

discolour *but* discoloration

Discovery Channel, the (TV)

discreet (circumspect), discrete (separate, abstract)

disease, legionnaires' disease, Minamata disease

dishonour

disingenuous (insincere)

disinterested (impartial), uninterested (not
     interested)

dispel, dispelled

dissension (*not* -tion)

dissociate (*not* disassociate)

distil, distiller

Distinguished Service Cross (DSC)

district attorney, district attorney Mike Fuhrmann

Ditto (trademark for copier)

dived (*not* dove)

divisibility, divisible, divisive

division, 6th Division

DJ (*not* deejay), DJs, DJing, DJed

DNA (deoxyribonucleic acid)

Dobson, Fefe (singer)

doctor (Dr., *but avoid* unless health-care
     professional)
     —doctor of laws (LLD)
     —doctor of medicine (MD)
     —doctor of philosophy (PhD)

doctor-assisted suicide, doctor-assisted death

docudrama

Dofasco Inc. (formerly Dominion Foundries and
      Steel Corp.)
dogcatcher, dogfight, doghouse, dog-tag
Dogs—Capitalize breed names derived from proper
      names except where usage has established the
      lowercase.
      —Dalmatian
      —Doberman pinscher
      —German shepherd
      —Newfoundland, Great Dane
      —St. Bernard, Irish terrier
      —*but* alsatian, dachshund, collie, pekinese,
      spaniel, etc.
Dominica (small Caribbean island republic)
Dominican Republic (neighbour of Haiti)
dominion
      —Dominion of Canada
domino, dominoes
Domtar Corp. (TSX:UFS)
donegal tweed
      —*but* County Donegal
Donnybrook (town), donnybrook (riot)
do-not-call list (for telemarketers)
donut—*Use* doughnut
dos and don'ts
Dosanjh, Ujjal (politician)
Dostoyevsky, Fyodor (novelist, 1821-1881)
dot-com (company, millionaire, etc.)
double-A-plus, double-A-minus (bonds)
doublecross, doublecrosser
double-decker
doubleheader (*one word*)
doubletalk
doughnut (*never* donut except in corporate names)
Doukhobor

D

Dow Jones (*no hyphen*)
>—Dow Jones Canada
>—Dow Jones industrial average, Dow Jones industrials

Down East

downhill

down payment (*two words*)

Down syndrome
>—Down Syndrome Association of Canada

Downtown Eastside (Vancouver)

Down Under (Australia and New Zealand)

Doyle, Damhnait (singer)

D'Oyly Carte

draconian

draegerman (mine-rescue worker)

draft (air, money, plan, military, beer)

draftsman

Dragon (sailboat)

Dramamine (trademark for travel-sickness medicine)

dreck

dressing room (*two words*)

drive (Dr.)
>—111 Sutherland Dr.
>—*but* 24 Sussex Drive (official residence)

drive in (*v.*), drive-in (*n.*), drive-thru (*n.*)

driver's licence

Droit, Le (Ottawa-Gatineau newspaper)

drop-down (*adj.*), drop-down menu

drop out (*v.*), dropout (*n.*)

drugstore (*one word*)

dry, drier, driest
>—*but* hair, laundry dryer

Dubai

duchess
>—Duchess of Cornwall (formerly Camilla Parker Bowles)

Duesseldorf, Germany
duffel bag, coat
duke, Duke of Windsor
dumbfound
Dunkirk (*not* Dunkerque)
Dunlap, David Dunlap Observatory (near Toronto)
durum wheat
Dutoit, Charles (conductor)
DVD (for digital video disc, *OK in first reference*)
DVR (digital video recorder, *OK in second reference*)
dwarf, dwarfs (preferred term for those with short
    stature resulting from a medical or genetic
    condition; *not* midget)
dye, dyeing
dynamo, dynamos
dysentery
dysfunction
dyslexia

E

E (not E!) network (specialty channel, formerly Star)

earl, Earl Spencer

    —Earl of Athlone

Earth—Capitalize when referred to as a planet.

    —The planets nearest the sun are Mercury, Venus and Earth.

    —The astronauts turned back to Earth.

    —down to earth

    —the good earth

    —heaven on earth

East—Capitalize regions *but not* their derivatives. Lowercase mere direction or position.

    —the East (region)

    —an easterner

    —Eastern Canada

    —an eastern Canadian

    —eastern Canadian markets

    —The snow moved east over Eastern Canada.

    —in eastern Quebec

    —East Coast (region)

    —east coast (shoreline)

    —where East meets West

    —eastern nations

    —eastern Europe (no longer a bloc)

    —Eastern Hemisphere

    —the Far East

East Block (Ottawa)

Eastern Townships (Quebec)

East India, East Indian — *Use* South Asia, South Asian

Eaton's (T. Eaton Co. Ltd., now defunct)

eBay (Capitalize lowercase names at the beginning of a sentence: EBay)

Ebola virus

ebook (for electronic book, *but* e-reader)

echo, echoes

e-cigarette

E. coli (bacteria)

e-commerce

economic action plan (Conservative government stimulus initiative)

ecstasy (*lowercase*) (*OK in first reference* for methyl-enedioxymethamphetamine)

ecumenical council

eczema

Edmonton Road Runners (AHL)

Edmundston, N.B.

EDT (*not* EDST), eastern time

educator (*prefer* teacher)

effect (*n.* — result); (*v.* — bring about)

effrontery (shameless insolence), affront (deliberate insult)

e.g. (exempli gratia; *avoid*)

Eglin (*not* Elgin) Field, Fla.

Egoyan, Atom (film director)

E.I. du Pont Canada Co.
       —DuPont (U.S.)
       —Samuel F. Du Pont (his usage)

Eiffel Tower (Paris)

Eilat (Israeli port)

Einstein, Albert (1879-1955)

Ekati (diamond mine in Northwest Territories)

El ("the")—ln Arabic names of individuals, the articles el and al may be used or dropped depending on the person's preference or established usage: Osama el-Baz, el-Baz (*second reference*); *but* Moammar Gadhafi, Gadhafi.

   For other names, the article is usually uppercase: Bordj El Kiffan (city in Algeria)

-elect, president-elect George W. Bush
       —*but* prime minister-designate Justin Trudeau

E

election day
Elections Canada
Elizabeth Fry Society
Elliot Lake, Ont. (*one t*)
ellipsis, ellipses
Elysée Palace
email, electronic mail
embargo, embargoes
embarrass, embarrassment
embassy, Canadian Embassy, Ukrainian Embassy,
 the embassy
embryo, embryos
emcee — *Use* MC
emeritus
 —Jean Duval, professor emeritus of history
emigrant, emigrate, emigration
Emmy, Emmys (TV awards)
emphysema
empire
 —British Commonwealth and Empire, the
 Empire
 —Holy Roman Empire
Empire State Building
employment insurance (*no caps*), EI (*second
 reference*)
enamour, enamoured (of)
Encana Corp. (formerly EnCana; TSX:ECA)
encyclopedia
 —*but* Encyclopaedia Britannica
endeavour
endgame *(one word)*
Energy Board, National (NEB, *but avoid*)
Engel, Marian (writer, 1933-1985)
England—Do not abbreviate and do not use as
 synonym for Britain.
English Canada, English-Canadian

enormity (wickedness), enormousness (size)
Enquirer, Cincinnati (newspaper)
enquiry — *Use* inquiry
enrol (*not* enroll), enrolled, enrolling, enrolment
en route (*always two words*)
ensign, the Red Ensign
ensign (rank, *no abbvn.*)
ensure (make sure of)
entomological, entomologist, entomology
entrepreneur, entrepreneurial
Environmental Protection Agency (EPA, *but avoid*)
Epcor Power Limited Partnership (Epcor Power LP
    OK in first reference)
epigram (witty saying), epitaph (inscription on a
    tomb), epithet (descriptive word or phrase)
EpiPen (trademark for epinephrine injector)
equator
ER (emergency room; *OK in second reference*)
Erasmus, Georges
e-reader (for electronic reading device, but ebook)
Erickson, Arthur (architect, 1924-2009)
Ericsson, Leif (Viking, about 970-1020)
erratum, errata
Eskasoni (Cape Breton First Nations band)
esker (post-glacial gravel)
Eskimo, Eskimos, *but use* Inuk, Inuit
ESL (English as a second language; *explain*)
Esquimalt, B.C.
esthete, esthetic
Eternal City
ethnic-Albanian (*adj.*)
eucharist (holy communion)
euro(s) (EU currency), eight euros, 8.1 euros, 26
    euros
Eurodollar (*no hyphen*)
European Court of Justice

E

European Parliament (legislative body of EU)
European Union (EU)
euthanasia (*preferred to* mercy killing)
even-steven
everyday (*adj., one word*)
e-waste (electronic waste)
exaggerate, exaggeration
exhilarate
exhort
existence (*not* -ance)
existentialism
exonerate
exorbitant (*not* exhorbitant)
expedite, expediter (*not* -or)
expel, expelled
Expo 67, Expo 86 (*no apostrophe*)
extemporaneous (*not* -eraneous)
extra-bill (*v.*), extra-billing (*n.*)
extracurricular
extraterritorial (*no hyphen*)
extravagant (*not* -ent)
ExxonMobil Corp.
eye, eyeball, eyebrow, eyeful, eyeing, eyelash,
        eyelid, eyesight, eyesore, eyewitness (*no
        hyphens*)
e-zine (Internet magazine)

F

Facebook

face off (*v.*), faceoff (*n.*)

faculty, faculty of law

FA Cup (Football Association Cup)
    —the Cup competition

Fahd Ibn Abdul Aziz (Saudi Arabia)
    —King Fahd *acceptable in first reference*

Fahrenheit, -20 F (hyphen, space before F, no period)

Fairmont Hotels & Resorts

fall (season)

fallacious, fallacy

fallible, fallibility

Fallopian tube

fall out (*v.*), fallout (*n.*)

FAQ(s) (frequently asked question(s))

Far East

farmers market *(no apostrophe)*

farm worker(s)

Far North

Farquharson, Charlie (character created by Don Harron)

fascism (philosophical attitude)

Fascist (party, member or government)

fascist trends

Father — *Use* Rev. as title for Catholic priest

Father's Day (third Sunday in June)

Fathers of Confederation

faux pas

favour, favourite, favourable

fax (*n.* and *v.*)

faze (disconcert), phase (stage)

federal
        —federal election
        —federal government

Federal Bureau of Investigation (FBI)

F

Federal Communications Commission (FCC, *but avoid*)
Federal Court
Federal Energy Administration (FEA, *but avoid*)
Federation of Canadian Municipalities (*no abbvn.*)
feedback (*n., no hyphen*)
feisty
fellow, fellowship
    —Nieman Fellowship
ferris wheel (*lowercase*)
fervour
fetal alcohol syndrome
Fête nationale (Quebec holiday on June 24, also St-Jean-Baptiste Day)
fettuccine
fetus (*not* foetus)
Feux follets, the (*no hyphen* — dance group)
fever, Lassa fever, spring fever
fiancé (man), fiancée (woman)
Fiberglas (trademark for fibreglass or glass fibre)
field, a polo field
    —Soldier Field
field marshal (*no abbvn.*)
fiery, fierier, fieriest
Fife wheat, Red Fife wheat
Fifth Estate, The (TV program)
fighter-bomber
Fig Newton (trademark for cookies)
Filion, Hervé (harness racing)
Filipino (male), Filipina (female), Filipinos
filmgoer, filmmaker
fiord
fire, fire department, firearm, firebrand, firebomb, firecracker, firefighter, fireplace
first lady (U.S. president's wife, *but avoid*)
first lieutenant (1st Lt.)

first ministers conference, meeting
First Nation(s)
First World War (*not* World War I)
50 Cent (rapper)
fivepins (bowling)
flack (press agent), flak (anti-aircraft fire)
flag-bearer
Flags—Capitalize the names of flags and ensigns.
    —Fleur-de-lis, Maple Leaf, Red Ensign, Rising
      Sun, Stars and Stripes, Tricolour, Union Jack
flair (talent), flare (flame, widening)
flak (anti-aircraft fire), flack (press agent)
flamboyant (*no* u)
flamingo, flamingos
flammable (*prefer to* inflammable)
flare up (*v.*), flare-up (*n.*)
flashpoint (*one word*)
flatcar
flaunt (show off), flout (mock)
flavour
fleet
    —the U.S. fleet (whole navy)
    —U.S. Pacific Fleet (formation)
    —Fleet Air Arm (Royal Navy)
Fleming, Sir Sandford (1827-1915)
fleur-de-lis (*not* -lys), Fleur-de-lis (flag)
flexibility, flexible
flight lieutenant (Flight Lt.)
Flight 132 (*capitalize*)
flight sergeant (Flight Sgt.)
floe (floating sheet of ice)
floodwater, floodwaters (one word)
Florida (Fla.)
flotation (*not* float-)
flounder (thrash about), founder (sink)
flout (mock), flaunt (show off)

F

FLQ (Front de libération du Québec)

flu (*no apostrophe*)

flutist

flyer (*not* flier), fly-fishing, flyleaf, flypast, fly swatter
(*two words*), flyweight, flywheel, frequent flyer

Flying Dutchman (sailboat)

flying officer (*no abbvn.*)

FM (frequency modulation)

FN (for Fabrique nationale) rifle

focus, focused, focuses, focusing

folksinger, folksong

followup (*n.* and *adj.*)

Food and Drugs (*not* Drug) Act

foofaraw

foot-and-mouth disease (*not* hoof-)

Football—backup centre, ball carrier, ball club,
blitz (*n.*, *v.*), bootleg, end line, end zone, field
goal, fourth-and-one (*adj.*), fullback, goal-line,
goal-line stand, halfback, halftime, handoff, kick
off (*v.*), kickoff (*n.*, *adj.*), left guard, linebacker,
lineman, nose tackle, out of bounds (*adv.*),
out-of-bounds (*adj.*), pitchout (*n.*), place kick,
placekicker, play off (*v.*), playoff (*n.*, *adj.*),
quarterback, runback (*n.*), running back,
tailback, tight end, touchback, touchdown

forbear (refrain from), forbearance; forebear
(ancestor)

force-feeding

Forces, the; Canadian Forces; the Forces (capped for
Canadian only)

forego (precede), foregone; forgo (go without),
forgone

Foreign Legion

Foreign Office (U.K.)

forerunner

foresaw, foresee, foreseeable, foreseen

foreword (in a book)

forfeit, forfeiture

forgivable (*not* -eable), forgive

forgo (go without), forgone; forego (precede), foregone

format

former
- —former King (Canada, U.K.)
- —former king (other nations)
- —former president George Bush
- —former prime minister Brian Mulroney
- —former Speaker John Fraser
- —former senator Robert de Cotret

Formica (trademark for a laminated plastic)

formula, formulas

Formula One (auto racing), F1 (*OK in second reference*)

Forrester, Maureen (contralto, 1930-2010)

Fort Chipewyan, Alta.

Fort Frances, Ont.

Fort Macleod, Alta.

Fort McMurray, Alta.

Fort Qu'Appelle, Sask.

Fortran (for formula translation)

founder (sink), flounder (thrash about)

Four Seasons Hotels Inc. (TSX:FSH)

Fourth Estate (press)

Fourth of July, July Fourth (U.S. holiday)

foxtrot (*one word*)

FPinfomart

fracas

fracking (*OK for* hydraulic fracturing on first reference)

francization (*not* -isation — *but preferably avoid*)

Franco-Manitoban

Franco-Ontarian

F

francophone (*lowercase*)

Francophonie, la (French-speaking equivalent of the Commonwealth)

freebie (free trip or other benefit)

freelance (*n.*, *v.* and *adj.*); freelancer (*n.*)

Freemason (*one word*)

freestyle swimming

french bread, french door, french fries, french-fried potatoes

French Canada, French-Canadian
—French-speaking Canadian

French Revolution

frequency modulation (FM)

fresco, frescoes

Freudian

Friedan, Betty (feminist, 1921-2006)

Frigidaire (trademark for appliances)

Frisbee (trade name)

Frobisher Bay — *Use* Iqaluit, Nunavut

Front, the (off Newfoundland)

Front de libération du Québec (FLQ)

frontman *(one word)*

front-runner

Fry, Elizabeth Fry Society

Fry, Hedy (MP)

Frye, Northrop (scholar, 1912-1991)

FTP (for file transfer protocol)

fuck — *Avoid* with few exceptions. (See *Stylebook*, page 18.) Use full word, not f*** or F-word (F-word *is acceptable if said that way in a quote*).

Fudgsicle (trademark)

Fuehrer, the (leader; used by Adolf Hitler)

fuel, fuelled, fuelling, fuel cell, fuel injection

-ful *(suffix)*, boxful, careful, cheerful, cupful(s), handful(s), harmful, spoonful(s), thoughtful, useful

fulfil (*not* fulfill), fulfilled, fulfilment
full time, a full-time job, working full time
fulsome (pejorative term, meaning excessive)
Fundamentalist Church of Jesus Christ of Latter
    Day Saints (This group, which embraces
    polygamy, *should not be referred to* as Mormon
    or Mormon fundamentalists, which implies a
    relationship with the Church of Jesus Christ of
    Latter-day Saints (Mormons).
fundraiser, fundraising, fundraise
fungus, fungi
furor (*not* furore)
fusilier (*no abbvn.*)
    —Fusilier Georges Coté
futile, futilely, futility
F-word (*used if said that way in a quote*)
FX (movie special effects; spell out *in first reference*)

G

Gadhafi, Moammar (1942-2011)
gaff (spar; fish-landing stick); gaffe (faux pas)
Gagnon, Christiane (politician)
gaiety
Gallup poll
Game Boy (two words); GameCube (one word)
Gandhi (*not* Ghandi)
Gap (retailer)
garnishee (*v.* — preferable to garnish)
Gastown (in downtown Vancouver)
Gatineau, Que. (formerly Hull)
GATT (General Agreement on Tariffs and Trade)
gaucho, gauchos
gauge
gauntlet (*not* gantlet)
Gaza Strip
gefilte fish
geiger counter
Geiger-Torel, Herman (opera, 1907-1976)
genealogist
general (Gen.)
> —chief of the general staff
> —Gen. Charles de Gaulle
> —Gen. William Worth

General—In compounds, hyphenate general when
it is the key word: major-general. Otherwise:
attorney general, auditor general, governor
general, secretary general.

General Agreement on Tariffs and Trade (GATT)
General Assembly (of UN)
> —*but* general assembly of the United Church

generation X, generation Xers, generation Y
> —*but* gen-Xer, gen-Y girl

genetically modified (GM, *but avoid*)
Geneva Convention (for one); Geneva Conventions
(all four)

G

Genghis Khan (c. 1162-1227)

Genie (movie award)

genius, geniuses

gentile

genus, genera

Geographical Terms—Capitalize regions but not
mere direction or position. Capitalize Lake,
River, Mountain, Strait, County, etc., when
preceding or following the specific term; *but*
lowercase the common-noun part of names in
plural uses: Ottawa and St. Lawrence rivers,
lakes Huron and Superior.

geographic information system (*lowercase; GIS OK
in second reference*)

George Cross (GC), Medal (GM)

Georges Bank (fishing)

George Town (Bahamas, Malaysia, Tasmania
—*most others are* Georgetown, *but check*)

George Weston Ltd. (TSX:WN)

Georgia (Ga.)

germane

German measles

Germany, Germanys

Gerussi, Bruno (actor, 1928-1995)

get together (*v.*), get-together (*n.*)

G-force

Ghanaian

ghetto, ghettos

ghoul, ghoulish

Gielgud, Sir John (actor, 1904-2000)

gigabyte (GB — *sing.* and *pl.* metric symbol)

gigahertz (GHz; *avoid or include explanation*: one
billion cycles a second)

gigolo, gigolos

gillnet, gillnetter

girlfriend, boyfriend

G

Girl Guides of Canada (association)
> —a girl guide, a guide
> —the Girl Guides, the Guides (association)
> —the Girl Guides movement
> —Brownie
> —Spark
> —Pathfinder

GIS (*Use* geographic information system *in first reference*)

Gitxsan-Wet'suwet'en

Giuseppe (Italian for Joseph)

gizmo, gizmos

gladiolus, gladioli

glamour (*but* glamorous, glamorize)

glasnost

GlaxoSmithKline

global positioning system (*lowercase;* GPS *OK in second reference*)

Globe and Mail, the Globe and Mail
> —*in bylines only, uppercase* the:
> By Greg Keenan
> The Globe and Mail

GNP (gross national product)

goalkeeper, goalmouth, goalpost, goaltender (*one word*), *but* goal-line (*hyphen*)

gobbledygook

god (idol)

God—Capitalize sacred names and the proper names and nicknames of the devil: God, Allah, Yahweh, the Almighty, the Father, Jesus Christ, the Son, the Lamb of God, the Saviour, our Lord, Holy Spirit, Trinity, the Prophet (Muhammad), Virgin Mary, Archangel Michael, Angel Gabriel, Satan, Lucifer, Old Nick.

Capitalize He, Him, His, Thou, Thee, Thine, You, Your in reference to the Deity. But lowercase who, whom, whose.

godchild, godfather, godmother

God damn, God damned (*not* goddam) — *Use with discretion.*

godsend

Gods Lake, Man.

Goebbels, Josef (1897-1945)

Goering, Hermann (1893-1946)

gofer

go-go

goitre

Golden Horseshoe (Oshawa to St. Catharines, Ont.)

Golf—birdie (1 under par), bogey (1 over par; bogeys, bogeyed), double bogey, triple-bogey 7, eagle (2 under par), par 4, par-4 hole, three-wood, No. 3 wood, hole-in-one, 1 over par for the round, shot a 1-over-par 73, Canadian Open, Canadian Professional Golfers' Association (CPGA), the Canadian Tour, Ladies Professional Golf Association (LPGA), Masters tournament, PGA Tour, Royal Canadian Golf Association (RCGA), Champions Tour (senior PGA tour)

gonif (thief; clever person; prankster)

gonorrhea

goodbye (*no hyphen*)

Good Friday

Good Samaritan

goodwill (*n.* and *adj.*)

Google, Googled, Googling (*uppercase*)

GOP (U.S. Republican party, *but avoid*)

Gore-Tex (trademark for fabric)

gorilla

Gosal, Bal (politician)

gospel, the Four Gospels
　　—the Gospels
　　—the Gospel of St. Luke

   —the gospel truth
   —a gospel singer
got (*not* gotten)
Goteborg (*not* Gothenburg)
Goth (Germanic tribe); goth (subculture)
Gothic (architectural style) *but* a gothic novel
GO Transit, GO train (for Government of Ontario)
Gould, Glenn (pianist, 1932-1982)
Gouzenko, Igor (Soviet defector, 1919-1982)
Government—Capitalize national legislative bodies,
      including some short forms.
      —House of Commons, Commons
      —House of Lords, Lords
      —House of Representatives, House
      —Bundestag, Diet, Knesset
   Lowercase provincial legislatures and their
      equivalents and county or city councils.
      —Manitoba legislature
      —Quebec national assembly
      —Toronto city council
governor, governor-in-council (cabinet)
      —Gov. Julius Mason
      —former governor Anne Lewcyk
      —Bank of Canada governor David Dodge
Governor General—Capitalize in all references to
      the Canadian incumbent; otherwise only as a
      title preceding a name.
      —Gov. Gen. David Johnston
      —the Governor General (Canada)
      —the governor general (others)
      —former governor general Ed Schreyer
      —governors general (*pl.*)
      —Governor General's Awards, Governor
      General's Literary Awards (*never* GG or GGs)
      —Governor General's Horse Guards,
Governor General's Foot Guards

GPS (global positioning system)

Grade 7 — *Use* numerals; *but* seventh grade

graffito, graffiti

Graham, Katharine (Washington Post, 1917-2001)

Grain—Capitalize variety names generally except
where usage has established the lowercase.
—Thatcher, Selkirk, Rescue
—*but* durum, garnet, Alberta red winter, No. 1
northern

grain grower

grain handler

Grammy, Grammys (record awards)

Granada (Spanish city), Grenada (island in the
Caribbean)

Grand Canyon

granddaughter, great-granddaughter

Grande Prairie, Alta.

Grande Prairie Herald-Tribune

grand jury

grandmaster (bridge and chess)

Grand Prix racing
—Canadian Grand Prix auto race

Grands ballets canadiens, les; les Grands

grassroots (*one word*)

Gray, Herb (politician, 1931-2014)

Greater Toronto Area (Toronto and surrounding
urban regions; GTA *but avoid*)

great-grandfather, great-grandmother

Great-West Lifeco Inc. (TSX:GWO)

Green Berets

Greene, Graham (novelist, 1904-1991)

Greene, Lorne (actor, 1915-1987)

Greenly Island

green movement (environmentalists); Green party

green paper (a tentative report of government
proposals)

G

Greenpeace Foundation
—Greenpeace V (vessel)
Greenwich Village
Greer, Germaine (feminist)
Greetings—Capitalize common specific greetings:
Merry Christmas, Happy New Year, Happy
Birthday; *but* season's greetings.
Grenada (island in the Caribbean), Granada
(Spanish city)
Grenfell, Sir Wilfred (1865-1940)
Gretzky, Wayne
Grey, Earle (arts award)
Grey, Earl (governor general, Grey Cup)
grey (colour)
Grey Cup (football)
Grey Panthers
grey whale
grippe
grisly (gruesome), grizzly (bear)
Grit (Liberal)
gross domestic product (GDP)
gross national product (GNP)
groundbreaking
groundcrew (aviation — *one word)*
Groundhog Day (Feb. 2)
groundswell (*one word*)
Ground Zero (New York City), ground zero (other
uses)
group captain (Group Capt. Ed Moir)
Group of Seven (artists), G7, G8 (countries)
grown-up (*n.* and *adj.*)
grow-op(s)
GST (*acceptable in first reference* for goods and
services tax)
guacamole
Guantanamo Bay

guardrail

guardsman (*no abbvn.; but* coastguardman)

guerrilla

guide, a girl guide

 —Girl Guides of Canada (association)

 —the Guides

Guinness, Sir Alec (1914-2000)

Guinness (stout)

 —Arthur Guinness, Son and Co. (Dublin) Ltd.

 —Guinness World Records

Guitar Hero (video game)

Gulf of Aqaba

Gulf Stream

gun, Bren gun, Sten gun

gunfight

gung-ho

gunner (*no abbvn.*)

gunnery sergeant (Gunnery Sgt.)

Guns—Rifles, pistols and other small arms are
 usually described in calibre, expressed in
 decimal fractions of an inch or in metric.
 The word calibre is not used with metric
 measurements. Shotguns are measured in
 gauge.

 —M-16 rifle, 75-mm gun, 12-gauge shotgun,
 .410-bore shotgun, .45-calibre automatic, 30-30
 rifle, .22-calibre rifle

gunship

gunwale

Gurkha (*not* Ghurka)

gurney

guttural (*not* -eral)

Gwaii Haanas National Park Reserve and Haida
 Heritage Site (Queen Charlotte Islands)

Gwich'in (aboriginal band)

Gyllenhaal, Jake and Maggie (actors)

G

gynecologist, gynecology

Gypsy, Gypsies (race of nomadic peoples; *prefer* Roma)

— *but* gypsy moth, gypsy cab

Gzowski, Peter (broadcaster, 1934-2002)

H—Four words and their derivatives begin with silent "h" — heir, honest, honour and hour — requiring "an": an honest man. Otherwise: a historic battle, a hotel.

Haagen-Dazs (ice cream)

habeas corpus (writ)

Habsburg (*not* Hapsburg) Empire

Hague, The

Haida (*sing.* and *pl.*)

hail, hailstone, hailstorm

Hailey, Arthur (novelist, 1920-2004)

hair's-breadth

hajj (Muslim pilgrimage)

hakapik (club used in seal hunt)

halal (food allowed under Muslim law)

half-, halfback, half-baked, half-hour, halfpipe (snowboarding), halftime, halftone (engraving), halves (*pl.*), halfway, halfwit, halfwitted

half, one-half
　　　—half a dozen
　　　—a half-dozen

half-mast (*not* half-staff)

Halifax Chronicle Herald

Haligonian (resident of Halifax)

hall, city hall, firehall
　　　—Massey Hall
　　　—Roy Thomson Hall
　　　—Toronto City Hall

Halley's comet

Hall of Fame

Halloween (*no apostrophe*)

Hamburger Helper (trademark for dinner mix)

Hamilton (specify if not Ontario)

Hamilton Tiger-Cats (*but* Ticats)

handcuff (*v.*), handcuffs (*pl. n.*)

H

Handel, George Frideric (composer, 1685-1759)
handful, handfuls
handgun
hand-held (*n.* and *adj.*)
handmade
H&R Block Ltd. (*no periods*; *no spaces*)
handshake (*no hyphen*)
hangar (aircraft), hanger (clothes, etc.)
hang-up *(n.)*
Hannover, Germany
Hanukkah
Hapsburg — *Use* Habsburg
hara-kiri
harass, harassing, harassment
harbour, Victoria harbour
hard line, hardline policy, hardliner
harebrained
Hare Krishna, Hare Krishnas
HarperCollins Canada Ltd. (publishers)
Harper's Magazine
Harris, Lawren (painter, 1885-1970)
Harris-Decima (polling company)
Harrods (London store)
Harron, Don (actor)
Hart Memorial Trophy, Hart Trophy (hockey)
hat trick
Havel, Vaclav (1935-2011)
Hawaii (*no abbvn.*), Hawaiian
HDTV (*OK in first reference* for high-definition
     television)
headdress
Headingley, Man.
headquarters (*usually takes a plural verb*)
Heads—Capitalize principal words in headings of
     tables, lists and other tabular matter.
head start

heads-up

health care (*n.*) health-care (*adj.*)

hearsay

hearse

heat wave (*two words*)

heaven

heavy water

Hec Crighton Trophy

Hegira, the (Muhammad's)

Heimlich manoeuvre

helix, helixes

hell

Hello (*not* Hello!) magazine

Hells Angels (*no apostrophe*), Angels (*second
     reference*)

helter-skelter

hemisphere
     —Western Hemisphere

hemophilia

hemorrhage

Hennessy, Jill (actor)

hepatitis A, B, C

herculean (*lowercase*)

hero, heroes (*pl.*)

heyday (*no hyphen*)

Hezbollah (Party of God)

hiccup, hiccuped

hide-and-seek, hideaway, hideout

hieroglyph, hieroglyphs (*n.*); hieroglyphic (*adj.*),
     hieroglyphics (*n., pl.*)

High Arctic

highbrow (*no hyphen*)

high commissioner, High Commissioner Lauren
     Chow

high definition *(n.)*, high-definition TV *(adj.)* (also
     HD or HDTV)

H

highlight (*no hyphen*)

high mass

highrise

high-tech

highway

    —the highway to Paris

    —Highway 27

    —Trans-Canada Highway

hijab

hijinks

Hill, the (informal for Parliament Hill)

hindrance

Hindu, Hinduism

hip hop *(n.)*, hip-hop music *(adj.)*

hippie, hippies

hippopotamus, hippopotamuses

Hirsch, John (1930-1989)

His—Capitalize His in reference to the Deity, His (or Her) Majesty, His (or Her) Royal Highness, His Holiness, His Grace, His Honour, His Lordship, His Worship. But use such terms of address only in quotations.

    —His Worship Mayor Phillips

    —and His Worship said ...

    —His Royal Highness, the Prince of Wales

Hispanic

historic (important or outstanding in history)

    —historical (about history)

    —a (*not* an) historical site

Historical Eras—Capitalize historical periods and events, including widely recognized popular names: Pliocene Epoch, Stone Age, Iron Age, Exodus, Ming Dynasty, Dark Ages, Middle Ages, Hundred Years War, Renaissance, American Civil War, Prohibition, Great Depression, Roaring '20s, Dirty '30s, Beer Hall

Putsch, Holocaust, Space Age, Me Decade; *but* ice age (no single period)
—21st century
History Television (Canada), History (U.S.)
hitchhike, hitchhiking (*no hyphen*)
Hitler, Adolf (*not* Adolph) (1889-1945)
HIV (for human immunodeficiency virus)
—HIV-positive
—HIV-AIDS
Ho Chi Minh City (Vietnam), Ho Chi Minh Trail
Hockey—blue line, face off (*v.*), faceoff (*n.*, *adj.*), goalie, goal line, goalmouth, goalpost, goals-against average, goaltender, left-wing pass, left-winger, play off (*v.*), playoff (*n.*, *adj.*), power play, power-play goal, red line, right-winger, short-handed (*adj.*), shut out (*v.*), shutout (*n.*, *adj.*), slapshot
Hockey Canada (governing body of amateur hockey in Canada)
hodgepodge (*no hyphen*)
Hodgkin lymphoma, non-Hodgkin lymphoma
Hoeppner, Candice (MP)
Hogtown (nickname for Toronto)
hold up (*v.*), holdup (*n.*)
hole, buttonhole, pigeonhole
Holidays—Capitalize religious holidays and feasts and all special times: Christmas Eve, Easter, Hanukkah, Yom Kippur, Ramadan, New Year's Day, Father's Day.
Hollinger Inc. (defunct)
Holocaust (murder by Nazis of six million Jews), holocaust (all other meanings)
Holt, Renfrew and Co. Ltd.
—*but* Holt Renfrew (no comma)
Holy Father (the Pope, *but avoid*)
Holy Grail (chalice Christ drank from); grail (any quest)

H

Holy Land

Holy See (Vatican)

Holy Week

home, homebrew, homebuilder, homebuyer, home field (*n.*), home-field (*adj.*), homegrown, homemade, homeowner, home page (*two words*), homesick, hometown, homework

homey (*not* homy)

Hong Kong Special Administrative Region, People's Republic of China (formal name, Hong Kong *OK in all references*)

honky-tonk (*hyphen*)

honour, honourable *but* honorary

hoodie (hooded sweatshirt)

hoof, hoofs

Hook of Holland

hoopla

horseback (*one word*)

Horse Racing—race card, racecourse, racehorse, racetrack, raceway.

hospital, hospital commission
  —Shaughnessy Hospital
  —St. John's General Hospital
  —Hospital for Sick Children
  —Laval hospital commission

hot, hotbox, hotcake, hotdog, hotfoot, hothead, hothouse, hotline (show, *prefer* open-line), Hotmail (trademark, *uppercase*), hotplate, hotrod, hotshot (all one word); *but* hot air, hot-blooded, hot cross bun, hot potato, hot spot, hot water

hotel
  —Royal York Hotel
  —Fairmont Hotel Vancouver
  —a Vancouver hotel

House of Commons (Canadian and British)
  —the House, the Commons

—the lower house (Commons)
—House leader Jean Roy (federal)
—the house (provincial)
—house leader Jean Roy (provincial)
hovercraft
—SRN-6 hovercraft
—British Hovercraft Corp.
HPV (human papillomavirus; *OK in first reference*
but include full term elsewhere)
HSBC Bank Canada
Hsu, Ted (politician)
HTML (Hypertext Markup Language)
hubbub
Hudson Bay
Hudson's Bay Co., the Bay (store), HBC (corporate
entity)
Hudson's Hope, B.C.
Hu Jintao, Hu *(second reference)*
hullabaloo
human papillomavirus (HPV *OK in first reference*
but use full term elsewhere)
Human Resources and Social Development Canada
humdinger
humdrum (*no hyphen*)
humongous
humour *but* humorous, humorist
Humvee (military vehicle), Hummer (civilian
version)
Huntington's disease
hurricane Hazel
Hush Puppies (trademark for casual shoes)
Hussein, Saddam (1937-2006), Saddam (*second
reference*)
Hutterites
hydroelectric (*no hyphen*)
Hydro-Québec (*hyphen*)

H

hyperlink
hypocrisy, hypocrite
hypothesis, hypotheses
hysterectomy
Hyundai Auto Canada Inc.
    —Hyundai Corp. (parent company)

Iacocca, Lee
I-beam
ice age (no single period)
icebreaker (*no hyphen*)
ice cream, ice-cream bar
icewine (*one word*)
iCloud, iPod, iPod Touch, iPad, iPhone (*Capitalize
    lowercase names at the beginning of a
    sentence:* IPod.)
ICU (*OK for* intensive care unit *in second reference*)
ID (identification, *no periods*)
Idaho (*no abbvn.*)
idiosyncrasy
i.e. (*prefer* that is)
IED (*use* improvised explosive device *in first
    reference*)
IGM Financial Inc. (TSX:IGM)
    —Investors Group Inc.
    —Mackenzie Financial Corp.
Ignatieff, Michael
Ikea (*not* IKEA)
Iles-de-la-Madeleine
ill, ill feeling, ill will; *but* ill-fated, ill-mannered,
    ill-starred
Illecillewaet, B.C.
Illinois (Ill.)
illusion (false impression), allusion (indirect
    reference)
imam, Imam Aly Hindy
Imax (big-screen movies)
imitator (*not* -er)
immanent (pervading, inherent), imminent
    (impending)
Immigration and Refugee Board
immovable (*not* -eable)
imperial, imperial measure

Imperial Oil Ltd. (TSX:IMO)

impetus, impetuses

implement (*n.* and *v.*), implementation

impostor (*not* -er)

impresario (*not* -ss-)

impressionism (school of art), impressionistic style

improvised explosive device (IED *OK in second reference*)

in, inbound, indoor, in-depth, infighting, in-group, in-house, in-law; break-in, cave-in, stand-in, walk-in, write-in

inaccessible (*not* -able)

inadmissible (*not* -able)

inadvertent (*not* -ant)

inauguration day *(lowercase)*

inbox (mail)

Income splitting (*two words*); *but* income-splitting policy (*hyphenate when used as adjective*)

income tax
  —income tax deduction

incompatibility, incompatible

Incorporated—*Use* Inc. in business names.

incorruptible (*not* -able)

Independence Day (U.S.)

independent, Independent (MP), Ind (*abbvn., no period)*

in depth, in-depth (*adj.*)

index, indexes
  —Dow Jones industrial average
  —S&P/TSX composite index

Indiana (Ind.)

indict, indictable

indigenous

indispensable (*not* -ible)

Industrial Revolution

Indy-car race

infallible
infantry, 4th Infantry Battalion
infinitesimal
inflammable — *Use* flammable
inflammation, inflammatory
In Flanders Fields (First World War poem by John
    McCrae)
information highway (*lowercase*)
Informetrica
infrared
ingenious (clever), ingenuous (frank, innocent)
inherent
in-line skating
innocuous
innovate, innovation, innovator
Innu (Aboriginal Peoples in Labrador)
innuendo, innuendoes
inoculate, inoculation
inquire, inquiry, inquiries
    —Cincinnati Enquirer
    —Philadelphia Inquirer
Inquisition, Spanish
inscribe (*not* enscribe), inscription
insignia (*sing.* and *pl.*)
insistence (*not* -ance), insistent (*not* -ant)
inspector, Insp. John Smith
install, installation
instalment
instant message, messaging (IM, *but avoid*)
instil, instilled
institute
    —Women's Institute
insure (cover loss)
intefadeh (Palestinian uprising)
intelligence quotient (IQ)

Interac (banking)
Inter-American Development Bank (IDB, *but avoid*)
Inter American Press Association (IAPA, *but avoid*)
intercollegiate (*no hyphen*)
intercontinental (*no hyphen*)
Intercounty Baseball League
interdependence (*no hyphen*)
interfere, interference
interferon (*lowercase*)
Interior, the (B.C.)
interleague (baseball)
intern (hospital)
International Bank for Reconstruction and
    Development (World Bank)
International Civil Aviation Organization (ICAO)
International Court of Justice (*no abbvn.*)
international date line
International Development Association (IDA, *but
    avoid*)
International Grains Arrangement (*no abbvn.*)
International Joint Commission (IJC, *but avoid*)
International Labour Organization (ILO)
International Monetary Fund (IMF)
International Space Station (ISS, *but avoid*)
International Telecommunications Satellite
    Consortium (Intelsat *OK in first reference*)
International Wheat Agreement, the agreement
Internet—Capitalize specific proper names.
    —Internet
    —World Wide Web, *but* the web
    —Adobe Acrobat, JavaScript
    —Twitter, tweet
    Lowercase descriptive or generic terms.
    —electronic mail, email
    —blog, chat room, cyberspace, domain name,
    home page, hyperlink, instant messaging,
    shareware

—web, web browser, webcam, webcast, web-enabled, webmaster, web page, web server, website

Use all caps for well-known acronyms and abbreviations.

—CD-ROM, FTP, HTML, HTTP (but lowercase in web addresses), PDF, RAM, URL

If providing an Internet address, follow upper and lowercase of actual address. Include www if appropriate: www.thecanadianpress.com.

If a company uses a variation of its Internet address as its corporate name, capitalize the first word: Amazon.com.

interpreter (*not* -or)

interracial (*no hyphen*)

intervene, intervener (*not* -or)

Intracoastal Waterway (*not* Inter-)

intranet (*lowercase*)

Inuit Tapiriit Kanatami (Inuit organization, means Inuit are united in Canada)

Inuk (*sing. n.* and *adj.*), Inuit (*pl. n.* and *adj.*)

Inukshuk (stone figure)

Inuktitut (language)

inundate, inundation

Inuvialuit (western Arctic aboriginals)

Inuvik, N.W.T.

Iowa (*no abbvn.*)

IPO (initial public offering; *OK in first reference* in business copy)

Ipsco Inc. (TSX:IPS)

Ipsos-Reid (polling company)

Iqaluit, Nunavut

IRA (Irish Republican Army)

Irbil (city in Iraq; *not* Erbil)

iridescent

Irish Republican Army (IRA)

I

Iron Curtain (outmoded term)
ironic, ironically (*use advisedly*; it does not mean coincidentally)
irrelevant
irreparable
irresistible (*not* -able)
irreverent (*not* -ant)
Islamic State of Iraq and the Levant (al-Qaida splinter group); ISIL, Islamic State militants, Islamic State fighters *OK on second reference, but¬† avoid using* Islamic State *in isolation*
island
    —Vancouver Island
    —the Island (*informal for* Vancouver Island and P.E.I.)
Ismailia (*not* Ismailiya)
Ispat Sidbec Inc. (former Quebec steel company; now Mittal Canada Inc.)
IT (for information technology; *spell out*)
Itar-Tass news agency
it's (it is, it has; *similar to* he's, she's)
    —its (possessive; *similar to* his, hers)
iTunes
IUD (*acceptable on first reference for* intra-uterine device)
Ivvavik National Park (Northern Yukon)
Ivy League

jackhammer
jack pine
Jackson's Point, Ont.
Jacuzzi (trademark for whirlpool tub)
jail (facility, usually provincial, where people are
    held temporarily or serve sentences of two
    years less a day)
    —county jail, jailbird, jailbreak
    —Don Jail (capped when part of formal name)
jalabiya (robe-type garment worn in Africa and the
    Middle East)
Javex (trademark for bleach)
Jaws of Life (trademark for extraction equipment)
Jaycees International, the Jaycees
Jean, Michaelle
Jean Coutu Group (TSX:PJC.A)
jeep (for the military vehicle), Jeep (for the
    trademark sport utility vehicle)
Jeff Russel Trophy (football)
Jehovah
Jehovah's Witnesses
    —a Jehovah's Witness, a Witness
Jell-O (trademark for gelatin dessert)
jerry-built
Jet Ski (trademark for personal watercraft)
JetStar
Jew (for man and woman, *not* Jewess)
    —Reform Jew
    —Orthodox Jew
jeweller, jewelry
Jiang Zemin, Jiang (*second reference*)
Jidda, Saudi Arabia
jihad (Arab noun for struggle to do good; often used
    to mean holy war)
jodhpurs
john (lavatory; prostitute's customer)

Johns Hopkins Hospital, University
Johnston, David (Governor General)
Joint Task Force 2 (Canadian Forces
      counter-terrorism response unit)
Jos. Louis (snack cake)
joual (Quebec dialect)
Journal de Montréal, Le (newspaper)
Journal de Québec, Le (newspaper)
JTI-Macdonald Corp. (formerly RJR-Macdonald Inc.)
Juan Carlos de Borbon
      —Juan Carlos I (king of Spain)
jubilee, Golden Jubilee, Diamond Jubilee
judge, Judge Kevin Ward
judgment (*not* judgement)
Juilliard School of Music
jumbo jet (wide-bodied jet plane, including the
      Boeing 747, Lockheed, L-1011, DC-10 and
      Airbus)
junior
      —John Jones Jr. (*no comma*)
Juno Awards, Junos
jury, grand jury
justice (usually reserved for appeal court judges;
      otherwise, use judge)
      —Chief Justice Albert Weisman, Justice Jean
      Dupont, Justice Sadie Kells (*not* Madam
      Justice)
      —Smith or the judge or justice in second
      reference
justice of the peace
      —justice of the peace Jean Isaac

Kabul, Afghanistan
Kaczynski, Theodore (unabomber)
kaffeeklatsch
Kahnawake (Que.)
kaiser (roll)
kaiser, Kaiser Wilhelm
kalamata olives
kamikaze
Kampuchea (now Cambodia)
Kandahar, Afghanistan
Kanesatake (Que.)
Kaposi's sarcoma (AIDS-related cancer)
Karadzic, Radovan
Karakatsanis, Andromache (Supreme Court of
    Canada justice)
karaoke
karat (gold), carat (gems)
    —14-karat gold *(hyphen)*
Karsh, Yousuf (photographer, 1908-2002)
Kathmandu
Kazaa
Kazakhstan
Kejimkujik National Park, N.S.
Kenora Miner and News
Kentucky (Ky.)
kerfuffle
ketchup
Kettle and Stony Point First Nation (Ontario)
keynote *(no hyphen)*
Keystone Kops
Keystone XL (pipeline)
KGB (acceptable in all references for the Russian
    words meaning Committee of State Security;
    but include a descriptive phrase such as
    former Soviet secret police)
Khachaturian, Aram (composer, 1903-1978)

K

khaki

Khan, Genghis (c. 1162-1227)

Khmer Rouge

Khomeini, Ayatollah Ruhollah (1902-1989)

Khrushchev, Nikita (1894-1971)

kibbutz (communal farm), kibbutzim (*pl.*),
kibbutznik (resident)

kibitz, kibitzer

kick back (*v.*), kickback (*n.*), kick off (*v.*), kickoff
    (*n.*)

kidnap, kidnapped, kidnapper

Kiev — *Use* Kyiv

kilo (*avoid* as an abbreviation for kilogram or
    kilometre)

kilobyte (KB — *sing.* and *pl.* metric symbol)

kilometre (km — *sing.* and *pl.* metric symbol, *no
    period*)
    —km/h

kilowatt hour (kWh — *sing.* and *pl.* metric symbol,
    no period)

Kimberley, B.C.

Kimberly-Clark

kimchee (Korean dish)

kimono, kimonos

kindergarten

King (of the U.K. and Canada), king (other nations)

King, William Lyon Mackenzie (1874-1950)
    —usually just Mackenzie King; King *on second
    reference*

Kingston Whig-Standard

Kinsmen Clubs

Kish, Nehemiah (ballet)

Kiss (*not* KISS) rock group

Kitchener-Waterloo Record — *Use* Waterloo Region
    Record

kitsch

K

Kitty Litter (trademark for cat litter)
Kiwanis International
Kleenex (trademark for paper tissue)
klieg lights (limelight)
Klondike
Kluane National Park
klutz (a bungler)
km/h (kilometres per hour)
Kmart stores (*not* K-Mart)
Knesset (Israeli parliament)
knick-knack (*hyphen*)
knight
     —Knights of Columbus
     —Knights of Pythias
know-how (*hyphen*)
knowledgeable
knuckleball
Kolkata (Indian city; *formerly* Calcutta)
Kool-Aid
Kootenai River (U.S.)
Kootenay East, West (B.C. regions)
Kootenay River (B.C.)
Koran — *Use* Qur'an
k-os (hip-hop artist)
Kostunica, Vojislav (Yugoslav politician)
Kosygin, Alexei (1904-1980)
Kouchibouguac National Park, N.B.
kowtow
KPMG LLP (Canadian arm of KPMG International)
Krakow, Poland
Krazy Glue (trademark for instant glue)
krebiozen (cancer drug)
Kreviazuk, Chantal (singer)
Krieghoff, Cornelius (1815-1872)
krona, kronur (Icelandic currency)
krona, kronor (Swedish currency)

krone, kroner (Danish and Norwegian currency)
Kuerti, Anton (pianist)
Ku Klux Klan
kung fu
Kurelek, William (painter, 1927-1977)
Kuujjuaq, Que.
Kwanlin Dun First Nation (Yukon)
Kyiv (*not* Kiev)
Kyoto Protocol (*but* Kyoto agreement, accord)
Kyrgyzstan (formerly Kirghizia), Kyrgyz (*n., adj.*)

La, Le—When lowercase in names, capitalize only
at the start of the sentence. Prefer "the" before
French names of associations and groups;
capitalize "le" or "la" when it is the first word
of the title of a book, song, play and the like.

L.A. (*OK in second reference* for Los Angeles; *use
periods*)

Labatt (part of Belgium-based Interbrew)
—Labatt Brewing Co.
—Labatt (*not* Labatt's) announced
—Labatt's beer

label, labelled

labour *but* laborious

Labour Day (*not* Labor Day)

labour sympathizer (union)

Labour sympathizer (party)
—Labour party

Labradorian (resident of Labrador)

Labrador Party

Labrador retriever

Lac de Gras, N.W.T.

lacklustre

Lac La Biche, Alta.

Lac-Megantic

Ladies' Home Journal

Lady Byng Trophy (hockey)

Lake—Capitalize as part of a proper name: Eels
Lake, Lake Huron. Lowercase in plural use:
lakes Erie and Ontario, Eels and Duck lakes.

Lake of the Woods, Ont.

Lake Shore Boulevard (Toronto)

lama (monk), llama (animal)

LaMarsh, Judy (1924-1980)

lambaste, lambaster, lambasting

Lamborghini

landau (horse-drawn carriage)

landline *(one word)*
landmine *(one word)*
Land Rover (trademark)
lang, k.d.
L'Annonciation, Que.
laptop (computer)
largemouth (bass)
largesse
larva, larvae
laryngitis
larynx, larynxes
lasagna
laser (for light amplification by stimulated emission of radiation)
Lassa fever
lasso, lassos
L'Assomption, Que.
Last Spike (driven into railway at Craigellachie, B.C., on Nov. 7, 1885)
Last Supper
Latin America *(no hyphen)*
laudable
Laumann, Silken (rower)
Laurence, Margaret (author, 1926-1987)
Laurier, Sir Wilfrid (1841-1919)
> —Wilfrid Laurier University
Lavigne, Avril (musician)
law
> —Law of the Sea conference
lawsuit
Lay—This is an action word; it takes a direct object: The gunman lays the rifle down, is laying it down, laid it down, has laid it down, had laid it down, will lay it down.
lay off *(v.)*, layoff *(n.)*
lead *(v.)*, led, leading

Leader—Capitalize as a semi-official title when used
with the name of a political party and directly
preceding a name.
—NDP Leader Jim Smith
—*but* party leader Jim Smith
—deputy leader Jean Roy
—former Tory leader Joe Clark
—House leader Tony Valeri (federal)
—house leader Claude Littlefeathers
(provincial)
—Japanese leader Junichiro Koizumi
leading seaman (*no abbvn.*)
league
—League of Nations
—National Hockey League (NHL)
—American League (baseball)
—Catholic Women's League
leap, leapfrog (*n.* and *v.* — *no hyphen*), leap year
Learjet (trademark)
LeBreton, Marjory (senator)
le Carré, John (author)
LED (for light-emitting diode (light); *OK in first
reference*)
Led Zeppelin
leery (*not* leary)
leeway
left, left field, left-fielder, left wing, left-winger,
left-field wall, left-handed pitcher, left-wing
politician (*adj., hyphen*)
Left Bank (Paris)
left-handed, left-hander *(hyphens)*
legation, Canadian Legation, the legation
Léger, Paul-émile (1904-1991, former Roman
Catholic cardinal
legion
—Foreign Legion
—Royal Canadian Legion, the legion

L

legionnaire

legionnaires' disease

Legislature—Capitalize national legislatures; lowercase others.

—Parliament, House of Commons, Commons, House *but* lower house; Senate *but* upper house; Congress, House of Representatives, House; Chamber of Deputies, Chamber; Knesset, Bundestag, French National Assembly.

—Quebec national assembly, Manitoba legislature, Newfoundland and Labrador house of assembly; legislature, house.

legislature member, member of the legislature

leitmotif

le May Doan, Catriona (speedskater)

lemon grass

lend, lent (*v.*), loan (*n.*)

lenience

Leningrad — *Use* St. Petersburg

Lent (season)

Leonardo da Vinci (1452-1519), Leonardo (*not* da Vinci) *on second reference*

Leopard 1 (tank)

Lepreau, Point

leukemia

Lévesque, René (1922-1987)

Levi's (trademark for a brand of jeans)

Lewiston Maineiacs (hockey team)

Lhasa, Tibet

liaison

libel, libelled, libellous

Liberal (party or member)

—the Liberal party

—Liberal Party of Canada (formal name)

liberal (philosophical attitude)

—a liberal education

liberty, liberty boat, *but* Liberty ship
> —Statue of Liberty
> —the Liberty Bell

library, Toronto Public Library, National Library
> (capitalize official names)

Libya, Libyan

licence (*n.*), license (*v.*)

licensed, licensee, licensing

Lie—This verb, meaning to recline or be situated, does not take a direct object: Trudeau lies in state, is lying in state, lay in state, has lain in state, had lain in state, will lie in state.

lie (*n.*), lie-detector

Liechtenstein

lieutenant (Lt.)

lieutenant-colonel (Lt.-Col. John Smith)
> —lieutenant-colonels

lieutenant-commander (Lt.-Cmdr. Stan Lyubic)

lieutenant-general (Lt.-Gen. Lee Ward)
> —lieutenant-generals

lieutenant-governor, lieutenant-governors
> —Lt.-Gov. Carole Pelletier
> —the lieutenant-governor said ...

life (*prefix*), lifebelt, lifeboat, lifebuoy, life cycle, lifeguard, life-jacket, lifeless, lifelike, lifeline, lifelong, life-preserver, life-raft, life-size, lifespan, lifestyle, life-support, lifetime

Life Saver (trademark for a brand of candy)

life-work

lightface (type)

light heavyweight

lighthouse, lightkeeper

light-year

likable (*not* -eable)

lime, lime-kiln (*hyphen*), limelight (*no hyphen*)

Limey (slang for British, considered offensive, *avoid*)

L

Limited—Use Ltd. and ltée (*lowercase, no period*) in business names.

Limited Partnership—LP (*no periods*) *OK in first reference* for business names: Fort Chicago Energy Partners LP.

linage (advertising), lineage (ancestry)

linchpin (*not* lynchpin)

Lincoln Center

line, line 2

lineage (ancestry), linage (number of lines)

lineman (football player), linesman (hockey official)

line up (*v.*), lineup (*n.*)

Lions, Gulf of

Lions Gate Bridge

Lion's Head, Ont.

liquefied natural gas (LNG)

liquefy, liquefier, liquefaction

liqueur

lira, lire (*pl.*)

Listeria (genus), listeriosis (infection)

Listuguj (Mi'kmaq band)

Liszt, Franz (1811-1886)

litre (l — *sing.* and *pl.* metric symbol, *no period*)

Little League Baseball World Series

livable (*not* -eable)

live-blog, live-blogging

living room

LLD (doctor of laws, *but avoid*)

Lloyd's (insurance market, shipping information)
　　　—Lloyds Bank (no apostrophe)

Lloyd Webber, Andrew (composer)

loan (*n.*), lend, lent (*v.*)

loan shark (*n. only* — *two words*)

loath (unwilling), loathe (despise)

Loblaw Cos. Ltd. (TSX:L)
　　　—Loblaw (corporate reference)
　　　—Loblaws store, Loblaws (retail outlets)

Local 14 (union)

Locations, Places, Sites—Capitalize the names
of important buildings, residences, historical
and battle sites, universities and colleges,
hospitals and hotels. Capitalize Union Station,
Grand Central Station as important buildings
but not when known by name of railway or
town: the Via Rail station, Leaside station.
Capitalize the names of parks, gardens, playing
fields and arenas. Lowercase post offices and
courthouses.

locker room

lock out (*v.*), lockout (*n.*)

lock up (*v.*), lockup (*n.*)

lodge, Orange Lodge
—the lodge meeting

log in *(v.)*, login (*n.* and *adj.)*

London Free Press

long (*suffix*), daylong, yearlong, weeklong *but*
hour-long, month-long

long distance, a long-distance phone call

long house

Long Island Rail Road

long johns

longliner (fishing vessel)

long-range, a long-range forecast

long-standing, a long-standing rule

long-term (*adj.*)

longtime (*no hyphen*, compound modifier)

Longueuil, Que.

loonie (dollar coin), loony (insane), Looney Tunes
(cartoons)

loophole (*no hyphen*)

looseleaf (*no hyphen*)

loran (for long-range air navigation system)

Lords, the (institution), lords (members), Lord's
(cricket ground)

L

Lord's Prayer, the
L'Orignal, Ont.
Losier-Cool, Rose-Marie (senator)
Loto-Québec (*hyphen*)
Lotto 6-49
Louisbourg, N.S.
　　　—Fortress of Louisbourg
Louisiana (La.)
Lou Marsh Trophy
lovable (*not* -eable)
lowbrow (*no hyphen*)
Lower Canada (name for southern portion of
　　　Quebec from 1791 to 1840)
lowercase (*n., v.*)
lower house
Lower Mainland (B.C.)
Lower Manhattan (New York City)
Lower Town (Quebec or Ottawa)
LSD (acceptable in all references for lysergic acid
　　　diethylamide)
Luftwaffe
lunch box, lunch bucket
Lunenburg, N.S.
Lutz (figure-skating jump)
Luxembourg
luxury, luxurious
Lycra (trademark for spandex fibre)
Lyme disease

M

MA (master of arts)
  —a master's degree
Macau
MacDonald, J.E.H. (painter, 1873-1932)
MacDonald, Flora
Macdonald, Sir John A. (1815-1891)
Macdonald, Man.
Macdonald, Angus L. (Nova Scotia politician,
    1890-1954; Halifax bridge)
MacDonald, Ann-Marie (writer)
Macdonald-Cartier Freeway, Highway 401
Macdonald College
Mace (trademark for a paralysing spray)
mace (staff of office; club), mace-bearer
MacEachen, Allan (politician)
MacGregor, Man.
Mach (speed, after physicist Ernest Mach)
machiavellian
machine-gun
    —submachine-gun
Macintosh (computer)
    —*but* McIntosh (apple)
MacIsaac, Ashley
MacKay, Peter (politician)
MacKenzie, Lewis
Mackenzie, Alexander (1822-1892)
Mackenzie, William Lyon (patriot, 1795-1861;
    grandfather of William Lyon Mackenzie King)
Mackenzie Highway, River, Valley
mackinaw (cloth, heavy coat)
mackintosh (coat)
Mack Truck (trademark)
MacLean, Ron (sportscaster)
Maclean's magazine
MacLennan, Hugh (author, 1907-1990)
MacMillan, Sir Ernest (1893-1973)

M

Macmillan Canada (former publisher)

MacNeil, Rita (singer)

Macphail, Agnes (Canada's first woman MP, 1890-1954)

Macpherson, Kay (feminist, 1913-1999)

madam (polite form of address; brothel-keeper)

madame (French title of respect)
  —Madame Roberta Duval (*no abbvn.*)

mad cow disease (*OK in first reference* for BSE)

mademoiselle (*no abbvn.*)

Madonna (performer), the Madonna (mother of Jesus)

Madras, India (now Chennai)

maelstrom

Mafia; Mafioso, Mafiosi (member, *sing.* and *pl.*)

Magazine—Capitalize when part of the actual title.
  —New York Times Magazine
  —Maclean's magazine
  —Time magazine

Magdalen Islands - *Use* Iles-de-la-Madeleine

Magna Carta (*not* Charta)

Magna International Inc. (TSX:MG.A)

Magnum (trademark for a cartridge), a .357-calibre Magnum revolver, a Colt Python .357

mail-order catalogue (*hyphen*)

Maine (*no abbvn.*)

mainframe

major (Maj. Alice Lajoie)

major-general (Maj.-Gen. Kevin Ward), major-generals

make up (*v.*), makeup (*n.*), makeover (*n.*)

malemute (dog)

Mallorca

Mamma Mia (musical, *not* Mamma Mia!)

mammogram, mammography (breast X-ray)

mandarin (civil servant); Mandarin (Chinese dialect)

manhattan (cocktail)

manhunt

Manila, Philippines
manila paper
Manitoba (Man.)
Manitoba Telecom Services Inc. (TSX:MBT)
manoeuvre
Man of the Year
man-of-war (warship)
 —Man o' War (racehorse)
mantel (fireplace)
mantle (cloak)
Manulife Financial Corp. (TSX:MFC)
Mao Zedong, Mao (*second reference*)
 —Maoism
maple leaf, leaves
 —Maple Leaf (flag, emblem)
 —Toronto Maple Leafs
Maple Leaf Foods Inc. (TSX:MFI)
Maple Leaf Gardens
March (*no abbvn.*)
march past (*n.* and *v.*)
Mardi Gras
marijuana
marine, marine corps
 —U.S. Marine Corps
 —Royal Marines
 —a marine, the marines, marine offensive, etc.
maritime
 —Maritime provinces, the Maritimes
 —New Brunswick, Nova Scotia, P.E.I.
 —The Atlantic provinces comprise the
 Maritimes and Newfoundland and Labrador.
Maritime Employers Association (MEA, *but avoid*)
marketplace
Mark III, Mark 46 (follow maker's style)
Marks & Spencer
marquess *but* Marquis of Queensberry rules

M

Marquis wheat

Marrakech (*not* Marrakesh)

Marseille

marshal (*n.* and *v.*), marshalled, fire marshal, parade marshal

Marshall Plan

martini

Martin Luther King Jr. Day

Martyrs' Shrine (at Midland, Ont.)

marvellous

Marxism, Marxist

Maryland (Md.)

Mase (rap singer)

MASH

Mason (member of Masonic order)

mason (person who builds with stone)

Masonite (a trademark for a brand of hardboard)

Mason jar

mass, low mass, high mass, requiem mass

Massachusetts (Mass.)

massasauga (rattlesnake)

mastectomy

MasterCard

master corporal (Master Cpl. Pierre Charest)

masterful (domineering), masterly (skilful)

master of arts (MA), a master's degree

master of ceremonies (MC)

Masters, the (golf tournament)

master seaman (*no abbvn.*)

master sergeant (Master Sgt.)

master warrant officer (*no abbvn.*)

matchup (*n.*), match up (*v.*)

matrix, matrixes

matzo, matzos

maximum, maximums

mayday (distress signal)

mayonnaise
mayor, Mayor Grace McDonald
    —the mayor of Ottawa
    —former mayor Ken Elman
    —acting mayor Ken Elman
    —the acting mayor
    —mayor-elect Ken Elman
    —Deputy Mayor Patrick Keenan (formal title)
mayoralty (*n.*), mayoral (*adj.*)
mazel tov (good luck)
MC (master of ceremonies), MCs, MCing, MCed, *but use only* when meaning is clear from context
McCarthy, Joseph (U.S. senator, 1945-1957)
McCarthy Tétrault (legal firm)
McClelland & Stewart Ltd. (publisher)
McClung, Nellie (feminist, 1873-1951)
McCrae, John (1872-1918, poet who wrote *In Flanders Fields*)
McDonald's Restaurants of Canada Ltd.
    —McDonald's
McDonnell Douglas Canada Ltd.
McDonough, Alexa (politician)
McEntire, Reba (singer)
McGraw-Hill Ryerson Ltd. (publisher)
McIntosh apple
    —*but* Macintosh (computer)
McLachlan, Sarah (singer)
McLachlin, Beverley (Supreme Court chief justice)
McLaren, Norman (filmmaker, 1914-1987)
McLauchlan, Murray (folksinger)
McLaughlin, Audrey (former NDP leader)
McLuhan, Marshall (1911-1980)
M'Clure Strait (in Arctic); named after explorer Sir Robert M'Clure (1807-73)
McPherson, Aimee Semple (evangelist, 1890-1944)
MDS Inc. (now Nordion Inc.; TSX:NDN)

M

meagre (*not* -ger)

Meals on Wheels

meat packer (*two words*) *but* meat-packing

Mecca (place)

—*but* a music mecca

medal, medallist

Medals—Capitalize specific names.

—Medal of Bravery

—the Military Medal

—a military medal

medevac (medical evacuation), medevaced

Medicaid (U.S. program of health care for poor)

medicare (government medical insurance plan in general), Medicare (U.S. health program)

medieval

Mediterranean

medium, media (*pl. —* except mediums in spiritualism)

Meech Lake accord

meerschaum (pipe)

megapixel (*avoid* MP)

Mehta, Deepa (filmmaker)

member

—member of Parliament (MP, MPs)

—member of the Order of the British Empire (MBE)

—member of provincial parliament (MPP — Ontario only, *but avoid*)

—member of house of assembly (MHA — N.L. only, *but avoid*)

—member of legislative assembly (MLA, *but avoid*)

—member of national assembly (MNA — Quebec only, *but avoid*)

memento, mementoes

memo, memos

memoir (*not* memoire)
  —*but* aide-mémoire
memorandum, memorandums
Mendelssohn, Felix (composer, 1809-1847)
meningitis, meningococcal disease
Mennonite
menswear, womenswear
mentally retarded — *Avoid* as sometimes considered
  offensive. *Use* mentally handicapped.
Mercator projection
Mercedes-Benz
merchant marine
Messiah, a messiah
Messrs. — *Use* Messieurs (before names)
meter (gauge)
methadone
Métis (mixed Indian and European ancestry)
metre (m — *sing.* and *pl.* metric symbol, *no period)*;
  but diameter
metrication (*not* metrification)
Metro Inc. (TSX:MRU.A)
Mexico City
MHA (N.L. only — member of house of assembly,
  but avoid)
Michigan (Mich.)
mickey (half-sized bottle of liquor)
Micmac — *Use* Mi'kmaq
micro (*prefix*), microbrewery, microsurgery,
  microwave, micro-organism
micronutrient, micronutrients
microphone, mic
microwaveable
midday
Middle (*not* Near) East
Middle Ages
Middleton, Kate (now Duchess of Cambridge)
  —Kate *OK in second reference*

M

Middle West, Midwest (U.S.)

Mideast

midget (*avoid; use* dwarf)

midshipman (*no abbvn.*)

midsummer (*no hyphen*)

midterm

midway (*no hyphen*)

MI-5, MI-6 (British intelligence)

MiG (for Russian aircraft designers Mikoyan and
     Gurevich)

Mi'kmaq (*not* Micmac)

mileage (*not* milage; for metric, *use* consumption or
     fuel consumption)

Military Rank—Plurals add "s" to the significant
     rank category, not to the qualifying word.
     —major-generals
     —lieutenant-colonels
     —sergeants major
     —regimental sergeants major

millennium (-nn-), millenniums

Miller, Glenn (band leader, 1904-1944)

Millett, Kate (writer)

millimetre (mm — *sing.* and *pl.* metric symbol, *no
     period*)

mill rate

Milosevic, Slobodan (former Serbian leader,
     1941-2006)

milquetoast (timid, after comic strip character Caspar
     Milquetoast)

Minamata, Japan
     —Minamata disease

Mini—Hyphenate unless the non-hyphenated form
     is established.
     —mini-budget, mini-play, mini-restaurant,
     mini-sub, but minibike, minibus, minicar,
     miniseries, miniskirt, minivan

minimum, minimums
minister

    —Energy Minister Joe Carney; Joe Carney,
    energy minister

Minnesota (Minn.)
mint, Royal Canadian Mint, the mint
minus, minuses
minuscule (*not* miniscule)
Minute Rice (trademark for quick-cooking rice)
minutia, minutiae
Miramichi River (N.B.), the Miramichi area
MIRV (for multiple independently targeted re-entry
    vehicle; always needs explanation)
misinterpret, misinterpreter, misinterpretation
mislead, misled, misleading
Mississauga, Ont.
Mississauga IceDogs
Mississippi (Miss.)
Missouri (Mo.)
Mitchell, Joni (singer)
mixed martial arts
Mixmaster (trademark for food mixer)
MLA (except Ont., Que. and N.L. — member of the
    legislative assembly) *but avoid*
Mladic, Ratko (Bosnian Serb general)
MNA (Que. — member of national assembly) *but
    avoid*
Mob (for Mafia), mob (other uses)
moccasin
model, modelled, modelling
Mogadishu
Mohawk (*sing.* and *pl.*)
Moldova (formerly Moldavia)
mollusk
Molotov cocktail

M

Molson Coors Brewing Co. (TSX:TAP.B)
—Molson Coors Canada Inc. (Canadian
division; TSX:TPX.B)
molybdenum (metallic element and commodity)
Moncton Times and Transcript
money, moneys
money laundering (no hyphen)
monitor
monkey, monkeys
Monroe, Marilyn (1926-1962)
monsieur (*no abbvn.*), messieurs
monsignor, Msgr. Ronald Thom
—Thom (or the monsignor) said ...
Montana (Mont.)
Monterey, Calif.
Monterrey (Spain, Mexico)
Montgomery, Lucy Maud (1874-1942)
month-long
Months—In dates, abbreviate except March, April,
May, June, July: Jan. 13, 1936; April 2, 1981,
was a Thursday; *but* January 2005, *no commas.*
moon
Moose Jaw Times-Herald
moral (*n.* — lesson, inner meaning; *adj.* — right,
just), moralist, morality
morale (*n.* — mental condition, attitude)
Moral Majority (*no* "the")
Morgentaler, Dr. Henry
Morissette, Alanis (musician)
Moriyama, Raymond (architect)
Mormons (members of the Church of Jesus Christ of
Latter-day Saints)
morocco leather
Morrice, J.W. (painter, 1865-1924)
Morse code
Moslem — *Use* Muslim

M

mosquito, mosquitoes

Mother Nature

Mother's Day (second Sunday in May)

Mother Teresa (1910-1997)

motocross

motto, mottoes

mould (*not* mold)

Mountain—Capitalize when preceding or following
    specific term.
      —Rocky Mountains
      —Mount Edith Cavell (*not* Mt.)

Mountie, Mounties (for RCMP)

Mount Sinai Hospital (Toronto)

Mount Vesuvius

mouse, mousey, mousier

moustache (*not* mus-)

movable (*not* moveable)

moviegoer

Movie Network, the

Mowat, Farley (author)

MP (member of Parliament), MPs (*pl.*), MP's and
    MPs' (*poss.*)

m.p.h. (miles per hour)

MPP (Ontario only — member of the provincial
    parliament) *but avoid*

MP3.com (company)

MP3 player

MRI (for magnetic resonance imaging; *OK in first
    reference*)

Ms. (*period*)

Much (formerly MuchMusic), *but* Much Music Video
    Awards

mucous (*adj.* — covered with mucus), mucus (*n.* —
    sticky secretion)

Muhammad (for founder of Islam and all other uses
    unless user prefers another spelling)

M

Muhammad Ali

mujahedeen (holy warriors, *pl.*), mujahed (*sing.*)

mukluk (deerskin boot)

mulatto — *Avoid*. Use black-white parentage or
some other description.

multi-, multicultural, multilateral, multinational,
multimillionaire, multimillion-dollar,
multimedia, multiplatform *but* multi-year

Mumbai (formerly Bombay)
—MUMBAI, India (placeline)

mumps (*takes singular verb*)

Murray, Anne (singer)

Muscovite (of Moscow)

muskellunge, muskie

Muskoka (cottage country in Ontario; *not* The
Muskokas)

Muslim (*not* Moslem)

must-have (*n., adj.*)

Muzak (trademark for recorded background music)

MV (motor vessel)

Myanmar (formerly Burma, *n.* and *adj.*); Burma can
be used in historical references

NAACP (National Association for the Advancement of Colored People)

NADbank (Newspaper Audience Databank)

naive, naiveté

Namibia (formerly South-West Africa)

Nanaimo Daily News

napa cabbage

naphtha

napoleon (French gold coin, pastry)

NASCAR (*OK in first reference* for National Association for Stock Car Auto Racing)

Nasdaq

Naskapi, Naskapis

nation, *but uppercase* as part of aboriginal name: Nisga'a Nation

National, The (CBC news program)

National Action Committee on the Status of Women (NAC)

National Aeronautics and Space Administration (NASA *OK in first reference*)

national anthem (*O Canada*)

National Assembly (national legislative body; Cuban National Assembly) *but* Quebec national assembly (provincial)

National Capital Region

National Chapter Canada IODE (official name of Imperial Order of Daughters of the Empire in Canada)

National Citizens Coalition *(no apostrophe)*

National Defence Headquarters (NDHQ, *but avoid*)

National Energy Board (NEB, *but avoid*)

national energy program

National Farmers Union (NFU, *but avoid*)

National Film Board (NFB)

National Gallery

national government

N

National Guard (in U.S.)
  —a National Guard unit
  —a national guardsman
National Hockey League Players' Association
National Library
National Organization for Women (NOW)
National Post, the National Post
National War Memorial (Ottawa)
nationwide (*no hyphen, but prefer* countrywide)
native peoples (includes Indians, Inuit and Métis)
  —native Americans
NATO (North Atlantic Treaty Organization)
Natuashish (Labrador community relocated from
  Davis Inlet)
Natynczyk, Walt (Gen.) (Canada's chief of defence
  staff)
nautical mile (1.853 kilometres)
Nav Canada
Navy—Capitalize Royal Canadian Navy when
  referring to force before unification in 1968
  and after name change in 2011. For other
  forces, lowercase navy when preceded by the
  name of the country.
  —Royal Canadian Navy until 1968 and after
  August 2011
  —British navy
  —Royal Navy
  —U. S. navy
  —a navy spokesman
  —U.S. 6th Fleet
  —Home Fleet
  —10th Destroyer Flotilla
Nazi (party supporter)
Nazism
NBC (National Broadcasting Co.)
N'djamena (Chad)

Nebraska (Neb.)

Negro, Negroes — *Use* black

neighbour, neighbourhood

Neilson Ltd., William (confectioner)

neoclassical, neoclassicalism

Neo-Confucianism

nerve-racking

Netanyahu, Benjamin

Netherlands, the

 —UTRECHT, Netherlands (placeline)

Nevada (Nev.)

New Age (spiritual movement)

New Brunswick (N.B.)

New Brunswick Telegraph-Journal

new Canadian

New Democratic Party (NDP)

New England

newfangled (*one word*)

Newfoundland and Labrador (official name of
 province)

 —N.L. (*abbvn.*)

New Hampshire (N.H.)

New Jersey (N.J.)

newlyweds

New Mexico (N.M.)

news, newsdesk, newsprint, newsroom, newsstand,
 newswire

Newsmaker of the Year (The Canadian Press)

Newspaper Guild, the; the guild

Newspaper Names—Lowercase *the* in names
 of newspapers: the Toronto Star; the
 Star; the New York Times, the Times. For
 French-language papers, write Montreal La
 Presse rather than the Montreal La Presse in
 first reference. In subsequent references avoid
 sentence constructions that juxtapose *the* and

le and *la*:: the La Presse editorial. Alternatives include La Presse said in an editorial, an editorial in La Presse.

New Testament

new veterans charter

New Westminster, B.C.

New World

New Year's Eve, New Year's Day *but* the new year (*lowercase*)

New York (N.Y.)
    —New York City
    —New York Thruway
    —New York state

Nexen Inc. (TSX:NXY)

Niagara Escarpment, Peninsula

Niagara-on-the-Lake, Ont.

Nichol, bp (poet, 1944-1988)

Nicholson, Rob (MP)

nickel (coin or metal)

Nickelback (performing group)

Nicknames—Capitalize nicknames generally.
    —the Old Man
    —Reds (for Communists)
    —the Queen City (Regina)
    —the City (London financial area)
    —Iron Curtain
    —Mike (Pinball) Clemons (brackets, not quotes); *but* Pinball Clemons (no brackets)

niece

Nielsen Media Research (TV ratings company)

night, guest night, ladies night

nightcap, nightclub, nightdress, nightgown, nighthawk, nightlight, nightmare, night owl, night school, nightshirt, nighttime, night watch

Nike

Nikon (camera)

Nineteen Eighty-Four (George Orwell novel *but*
   1984 for Michael Radford movie)

niqab

Nisga'a, Nisga'a Nation

nitroglycerine

N.L. (abbreviation for Newfoundland and Labrador)
   —ST. JOHN'S, N.L.; HAPPY VALLEY-GOOSE
   BAY, N.L. (placelines)

no, noes, no-noes
   —*but* She voted No in the referendum.

Nobel Prize, Nobel Prizes
   —Nobel Peace Prize
   —Nobel Prize in chemistry, physics, etc. but
   Nobel chemistry prize
   —Nobel Memorial Prize in Economic Science
   —Nobel Prize winner, laureate
   —Nobel Prize-winning researcher
   —the prize (*lowercase*)

no man's land

nom de plume, noms de plume

noncommittal

nondescript

non-existent (*not* -ant)

non-fiction *(adj, n.)*

non-Hodgkin lymphoma, Hodgkin lymphoma

non-life-threatening

nonplus (*v.*), nonplussed

non-profit (*n.* and *adj.*)

non-stick *(adj.)*

no one (*two words*)

Norad (North American Aerospace Defence
   Command)

Nordion Inc. (TSX:NDN; formerly MDS Inc.)

Nortel Networks Corp. (defunct)

N

North—Capitalize geographic regions but not their derivatives. Lowercase mere direction or position.

—the North (region of Canada)

—the north (of a province), northern Ontario, northern Quebec, etc.

—a northerner

—the northern territories

—northern natives

—Northern Canada

—the Canadian North

—the Far North

—the North Slope (Alaska)

—north of the border

—North-South dialogue

—the northern delegation

—the northern states

—The North defeated the South.

—North Atlantic

—Northern Ireland

North American Aerospace Defence Command (Norad *OK in first reference*)

North American Free Trade Agreement (NAFTA)

North Atlantic Treaty Organization (NATO *OK in first reference*)

North Carolina (N.C.)

North Dakota (N.D.)

northeast, northwest (*one word*)

Northern Hemisphere

northern lights

northern Ontario

northern states (of U.S.)

North Pole, the Pole

North Sea

Northwest Atlantic Fisheries Organization (*no abbvn.*)

North West Company
North West Mounted Police
Northwest Passage
Northwest Rebellion (1885)
Northwest Territories (*but* N.W.T.)
 —Northwest Territories council
nose, nosy, nosier
nosedive, nosedived
nostalgia, nostalgic
noticeable
Notre-Dame Basilica (Montreal)
Nouvelles Télé-Radio (NTR, the French-language
  service of Broadcast News)
Nouvelliste, Le (newspaper in Trois Rivières, Que.)
Nova Chemicals Corp. (*not* NOVA; TSX:NCX)
Nova Scotia (N.S.)
Nova Scotia Power Inc. (*no abbvn.*)
Novocain (trademark for a local anesthetic)
NOW (National Organization for Women)
'N Sync (musical group)
NTR (Nouvelles Télé-Radio)
nucleus, nuclei
number, number 2, No. 2
numskull (*not* numbskull)
Nunassiaq, N.W.T.
Nunatsiavut (region of Labrador controlled by Inuit)
NunatuKavut (formerly Labrador Metis Nation;
  pronounced Noo-na-too-ha-voot)
Nunavut (Canadian territory, *no abbvn.*)
 —Nunavummiut (resident of Nunavut)
Nuremberg, Germany
Nureyev, Rudolf (ballet, 1938-1993)
nylon

O

Oakland Athletics, Oakland A's

O&Y Properties Corp. (*no periods, no spaces* in O&Y)

oasis, oases

Oath of Allegiance (Canada's official oath)

obbligato

Oberammergau

Obhrai, Deepak (politician)

objet d'art, objets d'art

OCAD University (*formerly* Ontario College of Art and Design)

O Canada

Occidental (race; *avoid*)

occur, occurred, occurrence, occurring

Ocean—Capitalize with specific name.
> —Pacific Ocean
> —the Atlantic and Pacific oceans
> —an ocean wave

October Crisis (1970)

octopus, octopuses

Odd Fellows, Independent Order of (IOOF, *but avoid*), an Odd Fellow

Odesa, Ukraine (*not* Odessa)

odour, odourless *but* odorous

OECD (Organization for Economic Co-operation and Development)

Oedipus

off, offbeat, off-centre, off-duty, off-line, off-season, offshore, offside, offstage, off-white; blastoff (*n.*), blast off (*v.*).
> Similarly: cutoff, layoff, payoff, playoff, sendoff, standoff, stopoff, takeoff (all *n.*)

offence, offensive

office, county clerk's office
> —Home Office (U.K.)
> —Foreign Office (U.K.)

O

officer cadet (*no abbvn.*)
>—Officer Cadet Andrew Glenny

officer of the Order of the British Empire (OBE)

officers mess

O'Hara, Catherine (actor)

Ohio (*no abbvn.*)

oilfield, oilpatch, oilsands (*one word*)

Ojibwa (Indian — rhymes with way) (*sing. and pl.*)

OK (*not* okay), OK'd, OK'ing

OK (*not* OK!) magazine

Okalik, Paul (first premier of Nunavut)

Oklahoma (*not* Oklahoma!) musical

Oklahoma (Okla.)

Oktoberfest (beer-drinking festival)

old age pension

old age security (*no caps*), OAS (*second reference*)

Old Boys club, network

old-fashioned

Old Testament

old-time, old-timer

Olivier, Laurence (1907-1989)

Olympic Games, the Games
>—the Winter Olympics, the Olympics, the Summer Games
>—flag-bearer, medallist

ombudsman, ombudsmen, ombudswoman, ombudsperson (check with specific office to establish preference)
>—B.C. Office of the Ombudsperson

omelette

Ondaatje, Michael

One-Eleven (British aircraft)

one-time (*adj., hyphen for all uses*)

Onex Corp. (TSX:OCX)

online (all uses)

onstage, offstage

O

Ontario (Ont.), Ontarian
Ontario Health Insurance Plan (OHIP, *but avoid*)
Ontario Lottery and Gaming Corp. (*not* Corporation;
    OLG OK *in second reference*)
Ontario Power Generation (formerly Ontario Hydro)
Ontario Provincial Police (*but* the provincial police)
Ontario Teachers' Pension Plan, Teachers' (*second
    reference*)
onto (*prep.*)
OPEC (Organization of Petroleum Exporting
    Countries)
ophthalmologist, ophthalmology
opiate (a drug containing or derived from opium)

opioid (addictive narcotic compound)

Opposition—Capitalize when referring to the
    official Opposition. Otherwise, lowercase.
    —an opposition viewpoint, sat in opposition
    —the Opposition leader
opus, opuses
Orange Crush (trademark for pop)
orbit (*n.* and *v.*), orbital, orbiting
order-in-council, orders-in-council
Order of Canada
    —companion of the Order of Canada
    (recipients may use initials CC)
    —officer of the order (initials OC)
    —member of the order (initials CM)
ordinary seaman (*no abbvn.*)
    —Ordinary Seaman Alain Delisle
Oregon (Ore.)
Organization for Economic Co-operation and
    Development (OECD)
Organization for Security and Co-operation in
    Europe
Organization of African Unity (OAU)

Organization of American States (OAS)
Organization of Petroleum Exporting Countries
    (OPEC)
organize
Orient, Oriental (race; *but use* Asia, Asian)
    —an oriental flavour
    —Orient Express (train)
Orillia Packet and Times
orneriness, ornery
ornithology
orthopedic
Osbourne, Ozzy
Osgoode Hall (home of Ontario Appeal Court)
Otello (Verdi and Rossini operas), Othello
    (Shakespeare play)
Ottawa Renegades (CFL team)
Ottawa Rough Riders (former CFL team)
Ottawa 67's (hockey team)
Ouellet, André
out, outbid, outboard, outbox, outfield, outpatient,
    outtake (film); fadeout (*n.*), fade out (*v.*).
    Similarly: fallout, hideout, pullout, shootout,
    shutout, takeout, walkout (all *n.*)
Outaouais, western Quebec
OUTtv
Oval Office
overall (all-embracing)
overall, overalls (garment)
overbilling
Owen Sound Sun Times
Oxfam Canada
oxford (cloth, shoe)
OxyContin (trade name for oxycodone
    hydrochloride)
Ozawa, Seiji (conductor)
ozone

P

Pablum (trademark for a baby cereal), *but* pabulum (food)

pact, Baghdad Pact, Warsaw Pact

page 2, pages 1-3; p. 2, pp. 1-3 (*abbvn.* for tabulation)

Pahlavi, Mohammad Reza (shah, 1919-1980)

paleontologist, paleontology

Palestine Liberation Organization (PLO)

pallbearer (*one word*)

Palm Pilot

panacea

Panama, Isthmus of

Panama Canal

panama hat

Pan American Games, Pan Am Games (*no hyphen*)

panda (*not* panda bear)

panel, panellist, panelling

pantyhose

paparazzi (*pl.*), paparazzo (*sing.*)

paper-boy, paper-clip, paper-girl

Pap smear, test

Papua New Guinea (*no hyphen*)

paraffin (wax; in Britain, kerosene)

paragraph 2

parallel, paralleled, 49th parallel

Paralympics

paralyze (*not* -se), paralysis

paranoia, paranoiac, paranoid

paraphernalia (*pl.*)

paraplegic

parenthesis, parentheses

parimutuel (*no hyphen*)

Parisien Libéré (newspaper — *not* Libre)

park, Banff National Park, High Park

Parker Bowles, Camilla (*now* Duchess of Cornwall)

Parkinson's disease, Parkinsonism

P

Parks Canada
Parliament, member of (MP, MPs)
parliament
  —Parliament (national legislature)
  —parliament (provincial or regional)
  —parliamentary
  —Parliament Buildings (Ottawa)
  —Israel's parliament, the Knesset
parliamentary budget officer, parliamentary budget
    office (PBO *OK on second reference*); but
    Office of the Parliamentary Budget Officer
    (proper name)
parlour
Parmesan cheese
  —Parmigiano-Reggiano
parole, paroled, parolee
ParticipAction
partier, partygoer
Parti indépendantiste
Parti Québécois (PQ), Québécois's (*poss.*)
  —Péquiste (*n.*, *adj.*)
partisan
part time, a part-time job, a part-timer
party, Communist party, Green party, Liberal party
  —*but* New Democratic Party (NDP)
  —Parti Québécois (PQ)
Pashto (language in Afghanistan and Pakistan)
Passchendaele
passerby, passersby
pasteurize, pasteurizing
pastime
patchwork (*one word*)
Patriot (U.S. missile)
Pavarotti, Luciano
pavilion (*not* pavillion)
paycheque (*one word*)

P

payday (*one word*)

pay off (*v.*), payoff (*n.*)

payola

payroll (*no hyphen*)

pay TV, pay TV network (*no hyphen*)

PC (*OK in first reference* for personal computer)

PCB (polychlorinated biphenyl), PCBs

PDA (personal digital assistant)

pea, peameal bacon, pea soup, pea-soup fog,
    pea-souper (fog)

Peace Corps (U.S.)

peacekeeping

peacemaker

peacetime

peak (mountain, apex); peek (peer)

peccadillo, peccadillos

pedagogy

pedal (bicycle), pedaller, pedalling

peddle (to sell), pedlar (seller), peddling, softpedal
    (*not* -peddle)

pediatrician

pedlar (seller)

pedophile

peewee

Peggy's Cove, N.S.

pekinese (dog)

pemmican (dried meat)

Penashue, Peter (politician)

Penetanguishene, Ont.

penicillin

penitentiary, Kingston Penitentiary

Pennsylvania (Pa.)

pension, Canada Pension Plan (CPP, *but avoid*)

Pepsi, Pepsi-Cola (trademarks for a cola drink)

pep talk (*two words*)

Péquiste

perceive, perceived, perceiving

per cent, percentage, six per cent increase (*no hyphens*)

perennial

perestroika

perfunctory

perimeter (*not* -re)

periphery

permafrost (*no hyphen*)

permissible (*not* -able)

perogy, perogies

perquisite (perk), prerequisite (requirement)

Perrier (trademark for a mineral water)

perseverance, persevere, persevering

Pershing, Pershing 2 missile

Persian Gulf (*not* Arabian Gulf)

    —Persian Gulf War

persian lamb

persistence (*not* -ance), persistency, persistent (*not* -ant)

persona non grata

persuade, persuadable, persuasible, persuasion, persuasive

Petro-Canada (*hyphen; no abbvn.;* TSX:PCA)

petrochemical (*no hyphen*)

petty officer (*no abbvn.*)

    —chief petty officer first class (*no abbvn.*)

    —petty officer first class (*no abbvn.*)

PGA (Professional Golfers Association)

Phalange party (Lebanon)

pharaoh

phase, Phase 1 (*not* phase one)

PhD (doctor of philosophy)

phenomenon, phenomena

Philadelphia Inquirer (newspaper)

Philadelphia 76ers (*no apostrophe*)

P

Philip (usual spelling of first name)
—Prince Philip
Philippe
Philippines, the
—QUEZON CITY, Philippines (placeline)
—Filipinos (the people)
philistine (lowercase for someone lacking culture)
Phnom Penh, Cambodia
Phoebe
phoney (*not* phony), phoneys
phosphorus (*not* -ous)
photo-engraver, photo-engraving
phys-ed
piastre (*not* -er)
Picchio Pharma Inc.
piccolo, piccolos
picket (*not* picketer), picketed, picketing
pick up (*v.*), pickup (*n.* or *adj.*)
picnic, picnicker
piecemeal
pigeonhole (*no hyphen*)
pileup (*n.*)
pill (*lowercase* for birth control pill, the pill)
pilot officer (*no abbvn.*)
PIN (personal identification number)
pinch-hitter
Pinot Noir, Blanc (wine)
pin up (*v.*), pin-up (*n.*)
pipeline
—*but* TransCanada PipeLines Ltd. (*now*
TransCanada Corp.)
pixel, pixelate (divide into pixels)
pizzazz
placeline
—CORNER BROOK, N.L.
—MacGREGOR, Man. (for MacGregor)
—MACKENZIE, B.C. (for Mackenzie)

plagiarism, plagiarize

plainclothes police

    —police in plain clothes

plan, Colombo Plan, Marshall Plan

plaster of paris

plateau, plateaus

platoon sergeant (Platoon Sgt.)

platypus, platypuses

PlayBook (tablet computer)

play off (*v.*), playoff (*n.*)

PlayStation

    —PSP (PlayStation Portable)

    —PlayStation Vita

playwright, *but* playwriting

PLC (public limited company)

pleaded (*preferred to* pled for past tense of plead)

Plexiglas (trademark for an acrylic plastic)

PLO (Palestine Liberation Organization)

plow (*not* plough)

plummet, plummeted

plus, pluses

p.m., a.m.

podcast

pogey (slang for employment insurance)

poinsettia

Point Lepreau

Polanyi, John (Nobel Prize in chemistry, 1986)

Polaroid (trademark for camera, sunglasses)

Pole, the; North Pole, South Pole

Police—Uppercase when using the formal name of
    a force. Otherwise, lowercase.

    —provincial police, regional police

    —Toronto Police Service, *but* a Toronto police
    officer, Toronto police

    —Ontario Provincial Police (OPP)

    —*but* Quebec provincial police (*no abbvn.*)

—Royal Canadian Mounted Police (RCMP)

—Mounties (for RCMP)

—police chief

—police Chief Arnold Goldberg, Deputy Chief Emma Vokey

—police commission

—Quebec police commission

—police court, station

policy-maker

polio (short for poliomyelitis)

Politburo

Politics—Capitalize political parties, as Liberal, Labour, Socialist, *but* lowercase the words when referring to philosophical attitudes. Capitalize Opposition when referring to the official Opposition, the non-governing party with the most seats.

polka-dot (*hyphen*)

Pollyanna

polygamist (*n.*) polygamous (*adj.*)

pompom

Ponteix, Sask.

pontiff (for Pope)

Ponzi scheme (named after American swindler Charles Ponzi)

pope, Pope Benedict, the Pope (current pontiff), former pope, popes of history

poppyseed (*n.* and *adj.*)

Popsicle (trademark for ice on a stick)

pore (*v.* — study earnestly), pored, poring

Porsche

Portage la Prairie, Man.

Port aux Basques, N.L.

porterhouse steak

portland cement

Portuguese

postdate (*v.*), postdated cheque
postelection
post-game
postgraduate
Post-it notes (trademark)
postmaster general, postmasters general
Postmedia Network Inc.
post-mortem (*hyphen*)
post-season (*hyphen*)
post-secondary
postwar
potato, potatoes
potlatch (aboriginal gift, ceremony)
potshot
poutine
PoW (prisoner of war), PoWs
Power Corp.
power of attorney (*no hyphens*)
PowerPoint
powwow (*n*. and *v.*)
PR (for public relations)
practicable (can be done), practical (useful, functional)
practice (*n*. or *adj.*), practise (*v.*)
prairie
    —Prairie provinces
    —the Prairies
    —their Prairie farm
    —the prairie was parched in drought
pre, prearrange, Precambrian shield, pre-Christian,
    precondition, predate, pre-election,
precede, precedence (priority)
precedent (earlier instance)
pre-empt, preheat, premarital, preoccupy, prepaid,
    preschool, preschooler, pre-season, pre-tax,
    preteen, prewar

prefer, preferable, preferably, preference (*not* -ance),
    preferential, preferred

Premier—Use for Canadian provinces and
    territories, Australian states, France and former
    French colonies.
    —Premier Ann Bostwick
    —deputy premier Henry Miller (informal
    position)
    —premiers conference
    —former premier Roy Romanow
    —the premier of Ontario

première (*n.* and *v.*)
    —*but* a premier attraction

prerequisite (requirement), perquisite (perk)

prerogative (*not* perog-)

Presbyterian Church in Canada

president, President Barack Obama
    —the president said ...
    —former president George W. Bush
    —president-elect Barack Obama
    —Treasury Board President Tony Clement
    —Toyota Canada president Yoichi Tomihara

Presidents Day (U.S.)

Presque Isle, Me.

Presqu'ile Point, Ont.

Presse, La (Montreal newspaper)

Presse Canadienne, La (PC)

press gallery
    —Parliamentary Press Gallery Association
    —press gallery dinner
    —worked in the press gallery

pretence

prevalence, prevalent

prevent, preventable, preventer (*not* -or), preventive
    (*not* preventative)

price tag (*two words*)
PricewaterhouseCoopers
pricey
Priestley, Jason (actor)
Primakov, Yevgeny (Russia)
prime time, prime-time program
prince
    —Prince Charles, Charles, the prince; Charles, Prince of Wales; the Prince of Wales
    —Crown Prince Abdullah
Prince Edward Island, the Island (P.E.I.)
princess
    —Princess Anne, Anne, the princess
    —*but* the Princess of Wales or Diana (*not* Princess Diana)
Princess Patricia's Canadian Light Infantry
principal (main, most important), school principal
    —school principal Paul Chambers
principle (fundamental belief)
prison (use for federal institutions, not holding cells or provincial jails)
    —Oakalla prison farm
prisoner of war (PoW, PoWs)
private (Pte. Bob Lively)
    —private first class (Pte. 1st Class)
private member's bill
privatize, privatization
privilege
Privy Council (*uppercase*)
    —Privy Council Office (*no abbvn.*)
proactive
processor
Procter & Gamble Co., P&G (*OK in second reference*), P&G Canada
prodigy, prodigies, prodigious
professor, Prof. Normand Saint-Onge

P

program (*not* -mme), programmer, programming
   —national energy program
Prohibition (alcohol outlawed)
Promised Land
promulgate, promulgation, promulgator (*not* -er)
proofread
propaganda
propellant (*n.*), propellent (*adj.*)
propeller (*not* -or)
prophecy (*n.*), prophesy (*v.*)
Prophet, the (Muhammad in Islam)
prorogue
prospectus, prospectuses
prostate (male gland); prostrate (lying face down;
   overcome)
Protestant, Protestantism (religion)
protester (*not* -or)
province, provincial
      —province of Ontario (geography)
      —Province of Ontario bonds (corporation)
provincewide
proviso, provisos
p's and q's
psychedelic
psychiatric, psychiatrist, psychiatry
psychic
psychopath, psychopathic
psychosis, psychoses
psychosomatic
publicly (*never* publically)
Pulitzer Prize
      —a Pulitzer Prize-winning writer
pulley, pulleys
pulp mill (*two words*)
Punxsutawney, Pa.
Pusan — *Use* Busan for city in South Korea

push over (*v.*), pushover (*n.*)
push up (*v.*), pushup (*n.*)
Putin, Vladimir
putt (golf)
Pygmy
pyjamas
Pyrex (trademark for heat-resistant cookware)

Q

Qantas Airways
Qatar
Q-Tips (trademark for cotton swabs on a stick)
Quach, Anne Minh-Thu (MP)
quadriplegic
Quai d'Orsay (French Foreign Ministry)
Quakers (Society of Friends)
quandary
Qu'Appelle, Sask.
quarter-final *but* semifinal
quarter-horse
quartet
quarto, quartos
Quebec (Que.), Quebecer (*not* -ck)
Quebec City (*but* Quebec in placelines)
Québécois, Parti Québécois (PQ)
Quebecor Inc. (TSX:QBR.B)
Quebec provincial police (*lowercase, no abbvn.*)
Queen Elizabeth 2 (liner), QE2
Queen Mother (Elizabeth, 1900-2002)
Queen's counsel (QC)
Queen's Park
Queen's Plate
Queens Quay (no apostrophe)
Queen's University, Kingston, Ont.
question-and-answer, Q-and-A, Q-and-A's
questionnaire
question period (*lowercase*)
quiche Lorraine
quixotic (extravagantly chivalrous; from Don
    Quixote)
Quonset (hut)
Quotidien, Le (newspaper in Chicoutimi, Que.)
Qur'an (*not* Koran)

rabbi, Rabbi Stuart Rosenberg

raccoon, raccoons

race, race card, racecourse, racehorse, racetrack, raceway

racked (their brains)

racket (bat used in tennis, badminton, etc.)

racquetball (game)

Radio, Television Stations—Use this style: CFCF Montreal, CHUM-FM Toronto, CBC-TV. If a station uses another name, follow its style: Mix 99.9, 680News

Radio-Canada (*hyphen*)

Radio Moscow (*but* Moscow radio)

radius, radii

railway (*preferred to* railroad)
   —*but* Long Island Rail Road

railworker

rain, raindrop, rainfall, rainforest, rainstorm

RAM (random access memory)

Ramadan

rancour *but* rancorous

Rand (*not* RAND) Worldwide

R&B (rhythm and blues)

Ranger 4 (satellite)

rapt (absorbed, intent)

rarefy, rarefied

rational (sensible)

rationale (statement of reasons)

Ratzinger, Joseph (Pope Benedict XVI)

raucous (*not* -cus)

rayon

razzmatazz (*no hyphens*)

RBC Financial Group (TSX:RY)
   —RBC or Royal Bank (Canadian banking arm)

re-, readmit, reassess, recur, recurrence, re-examine, re-enter, reinstate, reissue, reopen, reorganize,

R

re-cover (cover again), recover (regain), re-lay (lay again), relay (pass on), reroute, rerun, re-sign (sign again), resign (quit), reunite, reuse, reusable

Re/Max (*not* RE/MAX)

Reader's Digest (*not* Readers')

ready-made (*hyphen*)

reality, realization, realize (*not* -ise)

Realtor—In Canada, a trademark and must be capitalized. Not a synonym for real estate agent. It identifies members of the Canadian Real Estate Association and the (U.S.) National Association of Realtors, which includes agents or brokers, *but* also property managers, developers and other real estate professionals.

REAL Women

rearguard

rebut, refute (prove wrong; *use with care*)

recoilless

Red (Communist, *but avoid*)

Redblacks (Ottawa CFL team)

Red Chamber (nickname for Canada's Senate chamber; *avoid*)

Red Cross, Red Cross Society, Red Crescent —a Red Cross campaign

redneck (rustic, poor white)

Reeves, Keanu

refer, referred

referendum, referendums

Reformation

reformatory, Guelph reformatory

refuel, refuelled

refute, rebut (prove wrong; *use with care*)

reggae

regiment, 24th Regiment

regimental sergeant major (Regimental Sgt. Maj.) —regimental sergeants major (*no abbvn.*)

Regina Leader-Post

region, Peel Region

registered education savings plan (RESP)

registered retirement savings plan (RRSP)

reign (rule), rein (leather strap, symbol of power)

Religion—Capitalize names of religions and
denominations.

> —American Lutheran Church
>
> —Anglican Church of Canada
>
> —Baha'i faith
>
> —Buddhism, Buddhist
>
> —Church of Christ, Scientist (also Christian
> Science Church)
>
> —Church of Jesus Christ of Latter-day Saints
>
> —Greek Orthodox Church
>
> —Hinduism, Hindu
>
> —Islam, Muslim
>
> —Jehovah's Witnesses
>
> —Judaism (Orthodox, Reform, Conservative)
>
> —Pentecostal Assembly
>
> —Presbyterian Church in Canada
>
> —Roman Catholic Church
>
> —Seventh-day Adventist
>
> —Ukrainian Orthodox Church
>
> —United Church of Canada

relinquish

R.E.M. (musical group)

Remembrance Day (Nov. 11)

reminiscent

removable (*not* -eable)

remuneration

Renaissance (historic period), a renaissance of
painting (general sense)

rendezvous (*n.* and *v.*)

renowned

repechage (rowing)

R

repel, repellent
repent, repentance, repentant
repertoire, repertory
representative (U.S. Congress)
>—Rep. Donna Hooper
>—Rep. Robert Brown

reprieve
republic, Fifth Republic
>—Republic of Ireland
>—the Irish republic

Republican (party or member)
>—Republican party (U.S.)

republican (philosophical attitude)
requiem, requiem mass
research and development, R&D (*no periods*)
Research In Motion Ltd. (RIM) - now BlackBerry
reserve (*preferred to* reservation for aboriginal lands
>in Canada), the Chippewa reserve

re-sign (sign again), resign (quit)
resistance, resistibility, resistible (*not* -able)
RESOLUTE, Nunavut (placeline), not Resolute Bay
respectability, respectable
restaurateur (*not* restauranteur)
resumé
resuscitate
retired, retired brigadier Pat Turner
Reuters, Reuters news agency
reverend
>—Rev. Alan Cross (Protestant and RC; Cross *on
>second reference*)

reverse, reversible
revolution, American Revolution
revolutions per minute (r.p.m.)
Reye's syndrome
Rh (for Rhesus) factor, Rh positive, Rh negative
rhinoceros (*sing.* and *pl.*)

Rhode Island (R.I.)
Rhodes Scholar, Scholarship
rhododendron
Rice, Condoleezza
Richler, Mordecai (author, 1931-2001)
Richter scale
Richthofen, Baron von (Red Baron, 1892-1918)
ricochet, ricocheted
Rideau Hall
ride-hailing, ride-booking (*not* ride-sharing)
rifleman (*no abbvn.*)
     —Rifleman Andrew Coates
right, right field, right-fielder, right wing,
right-handed, right-hander (*hyphen*)
right-winger; right-field wall, right-handed pitcher,
     right-wing politician (*adj., hyphen*)
rigor mortis
rigour *but* rigorous
ringtone (*one word*)
Rio de Janeiro
Rio Tinto Alcan
rip off (*v.*), ripoff (*n.*)
river, St. Lawrence River
Riyadh
RJR-Macdonald Inc. — now JTI-Macdonald Corp.
Road—Capitalize when used with names,
     abbreviate in numbered street addresses.
     —along Kingston Road
     —10 Scott Rd. E.
roadblock (*one word*), road map (*two words*)
robocall, robocalling (*no hyphen*)
Rock, the (informal for Newfoundland or Gibraltar)
Rockefeller Center
rock 'n' roll
rococo
Rodrigue (given name — *not* -que)

Rogers Centre, Toronto (formerly SkyDome)

Rogers Communications Inc. (TSX:RCI.B)

   —Rogers Cable

   —Rogers Media

   —Rogers Video

   —Rogers Wireless

Rogers Pass, B.C.

rollcall (*one word*)

Rollerblades (trademark for in-line skates),
   Rollerblading (*but use* in-line skating)

roller-coaster, roller derby, roller-skate (*v.*), roller
   skates

rollover (*n.*)

Rolls-Royce Ltd., a Rolls-Royce

Roll up the Rim (Tim Hortons contest)

Rolodex

roly-poly (*hyphen*)

ROM (read only memory)

Roma (*preferred to* Gypsy)

Roman Catholic (Roman may be dropped only if
   reference is obvious)

Romanesque

Romania (*not* Rumania)

roman numerals, type

Roman Numerals—Use roman numerals to
   indicate sequence for people and animals and
   in proper names where specified. Otherwise
   prefer arabic numerals as easier to grasp.
   —Pope Benedict XVI, Henry VIII, *The
   Godfather, Part II*

roof, roofs

room, Room 4, Oak Room
   —in the assembly room

Rorschach test

Rosh Hashanah

Rothmans Inc. (TSX:ROC)

Rothschild

Rottweiler

roundtable (*one word, n.* and *adj.*)

roundup (*n.*), round up (*v.*)

Royal Air Force (Britain)

royal assent

Royal Canadian Air Force (until 1968 and after
      August 2011)

Royal Canadian Mint, the mint

Royal Canadian Mounted Police (RCMP)
     —RCMP musical ride
     —the Mounties

Royal Canadian Navy (until 1968 and after August
      2011)

Royal Family (British), royal family (other nations)

Royal Ontario Museum (ROM, *but avoid)*

royal tour, visit

royalty

Roy Thomson Hall (Toronto)

r.p.m. (revolutions per minute)

RRSP (registered retirement savings plan)

RSS (*OK in first reference* for Really Simple
     Syndication)

ruble

Rugby—centre, fly half, fullback, lineout, scrum
     half, Test match, try, tries

rumour

runner-up, runners-up

run-off, run-up
   —*but* spring runoff (no hyphen)

rural route
     —RR 2, Newmarket

rush hour, rush-hour traffic

R

Russia
RV (for recreational vehicle)
Rwanda
Ryerson University (Toronto)

'S—To denote the possessive add 's to singular
and plural nouns not ending in "s": mother's
purse, women's shoes, alumni's gifts. Add it
to singular nouns ending in "s" to indicate a
sis or siz sound: the boss's secretary, Strauss's
waltzes, Duplessis's cabinet. But names ending
with an -iz sound and classical names ending
in "s" often take the apostrophe only: Bridges'
ideas, Socrates' plays.

Sabbath

saccharin (*n.*), saccharine (*adj.*)

sacrilegious

Saddam Hussein (1937-2006); Saddam *in second
reference*

Sadler's Wells Ballet

Sailboats—Capitalize names of classes of racing
and pleasure craft.

—Tornado, International Europe

Sainte-Marie, Buffy (singer-composer)

Sainte-Marie among the Hurons (Midland, Ont.)

Saint John, N.B.

Saint Mary's University (Halifax)

salability, salable (*not* -eable)

Salchow, triple Salchow (figure-skating jump)

salmonella

SALT (for strategic arms limitation talks)

Salvadoran

Salvation Army, the Army, a Salvationist

salvo, salvos (*pl.*)

SAM (for surface-to-air missile)

Samaritan, Good

Sanaa, Yemen

sanatorium, sanatoriums

sanctimonious

Sanforized (trademark for material that won't shrink)

San Francisco 49ers (*no apostrophe*)

S

Sanka (trademark for a decaffeinated coffee)
sapper (*no abbvn.*)
    —Sapper John Flynn
Sarajevo
Saran Wrap (trademark for a plastic film)
SARS (severe acute respiratory syndrome, *OK in first reference)*
Saskatchewan (*not* Regina) Roughriders (*one word*)
Saskatchewan (Sask.)
Saskatchewan Party
    —Sask. Party *OK if abbreviation needed*
saskatoon (berry)
Saskatoon StarPhoenix
sasquatch (mysterious ape-like creature)
Satan, satanic, Satanism
Sault Ste. Marie, Ont. and Mich.
    —the Sault (*not* the Soo)
    —*but* Soo Greyhounds hockey team
    —the Sault Star
Savile Row (London)
saviour, Saviour (Christ)
savory (herb)
savour, savoury (flavour)
saxophone
scare, scary, scarier
scarf, scarves
scarlet fever
Scene 2, the second scene
sceptic — *Use* skeptic
Schafer, R. Murray (composer)
Scheer, Andrew (MP)
Schefferville, Que.
schizophrenia, schizophrenic
scholar, Rhodes Scholar, Scholarship
School—Capitalize when using proper name.
    —Leaside High School

—Our Lady of Sorrows School
—London School of Economics
—University of Toronto Schools
—Royal York Academy *(proper name)* but Royal York high school
—Kingslake Public School *(proper name)* but Kingslake elementary school
—the McGill medical school
—day school, private school
—Sunday school
—school board, schoolbook, schoolboy, school bus, schoolchildren, schoolgirl, school guard, school teacher, school trustee, schoolyard

Schumann, Robert (composer, 1810-1856)

Schwartz, Gerry

Schwarzenegger, Arnold

Scientology, Church of Scientology

Scorsese, Martin (film director)

Scotch Tape (trademark for sticky tape)

Scotch whisky, *but* lowercase when used alone: scotch

Scotiabank, Scotiabank Group (TSX:BNS)
    —Bank of Nova Scotia (legal name)
    —ScotiaMcLeod (retail brokerage)
    —Scotia Capital Inc. (corporate investment arm)

Scotsman (*not* Scotchman)

Scots or Scottish (*not* Scotch)

scout
    —Scouts Canada
    —the Scouts (association)
    —a scout
    —eagle scout (U.S.)
    —Beaver
    —Cub

—Chief Scout's Award
—Venturer Scout, Venturers
Scrabble (trademark for a word game)
Screech (rum)
Scripture (Bible)
S-curve
scuttlebutt (*no hyphen*)
Sea—Capitalize when preceding or following the
specific term.
—Sea of Galilee
—Black Sea
Sea-Doo (trademark for a brand of personal
watercraft)
Seafarers International Union of Canada (SIU)
SEAL (U.S. navy)
seaman
—able seaman (*no abbvn.*)
—leading seaman (*no abbvn.*)
—ordinary seaman (*no abbvn.*)
Sears Canada Inc. (TSX:SCC)
—a Sears store, Sears
Seasons—Lowercase for spring, summer, fall or
autumn, winter
season's greetings
seatbelt (*one word*)
SEATO (for Southeast Asia Treaty Organization)
seaway, St. Lawrence Seaway
—St. Lawrence Seaway Authority
—St. Lawrence Seaway Development Corp.
second lieutenant (2nd Lt. Marie Demers)
Second World War (*not* World War II)
secretary general (*no hyphen*)
Section 23, Sec. 5
Security Council (UN)
seder
Seeing Eye (trademark for guide dog)

seigneur, seigniory

semi, semi-annual, semi-automatic, semicircle,
semicolon, semifinal (*but* quarter-final),
semifinalist, semi-invalid, semi-official,
semitransparent, semitropical, semi-weekly

Semite, Semitism, anti-Semitism

Senate (national legislature); senate (state legislature)
—the university senate

senator (Canada and U.S.)
—Sen. Edward Kennedy, Sen. Nancy Greene
—former senator Robert de Cotret

senior chief petty officer (*no abbvn.*)

sensual (gratifying to the body, especially sexually),
sensuous (appealing to the senses, especially
through beauty)

separate school, school board

Sept. 11 (day of terrorist attacks in United States; *not*
September 11), 9/11

Serb (*n.*), Serbian (*adj.*)

Serbia and Montenegro (formerly Yugoslavia)
—SERBIA-MONTENEGRO (placelines)

sergeant (Sgt. Margaret Bonotto)
—staff sergeant (Staff Sgt. Margaret Bonotto)

sergeant-at-arms

sergeant first class (Sgt. 1st Class)

sergeant major (Sgt. Maj. Fred Tylee)
—regimental sergeant major (Regimental Sgt.
Maj.)
—sergeants major (*pl.*)

series (*generally lowercase*)
—*but* World Series, the Series, Little League
World Series

set up (*v.*), setup (*n.*)

Seventh-day Adventist

7Up (soft drink)
—Seven-Up (corporate references)

severe acute respiratory syndrome (SARS *OK in first reference)*

sewage (waste), sewerage (drainage)

Sex and the City (TV show, *not Sex in the City*)

sextet

sexually transmitted disease (STD *but avoid*)

Shaffer, Paul (bandleader)

shakable (*not* -eable)

shake down (*v.*), shakedown (*n.* and *adj.*)

shake out (v.), shakeout (*n.* and *adj.*)

Shakespeare, Shakespearean

shake up (*v.*), shakeup (*n.*)

shaky, shakier, shakiness

shalom (greeting)

shaman, shamans (*pl.*), Shamanism

shanghai (*v.*), shanghaied, shanghaiing

Shangri-La

shanty, shanties

Sharansky, Natan

Shariah (Muslim code of religious law)

Shaw Communications Inc. (TSX:SJR.B)

sheik (*not* shiek)

shellac, shellacking

shemozzle (commotion)

sheriff, Sheriff Anton Gerber

Sheshatshiu, Labrador (formerly Sheshatsheit)

Shiite Muslim

Shippagan, N.B. (*not* Shippegan)

shipwreck (*no hyphen*)

Shirleys Bay, Ont. (*no apostrophe*)

shish kebab

shiva

shivaree (friendly invasion of newlyweds' home)

shlemiel (foolish, unlucky person)

shlep (to drag)

shlock (shoddy)

shmaltz (sentimentality)
shmo (a fool, a clumsy person)
shmooz (chat)
shnook (a patsy)
shnorrer (a moocher, panhandler)
shoo-in
shoot out (*v.*), shootout (*n.*)
Shoppers Drug Mart Corp. (TSX:SC)
shoptalk
short list (*n.*) shortlist (*v.*)
shortwave (broadcasting)
shotgun (*one word*)
shot put (*two words*)
show, flower show, horse show
shtick (a gimmick; clowning)
shut out (*v.*), shutout (*n.*)
siamese twins (*use* joined twins or description: babies born attached at the hips)
side-effect
Sidney, B.C.
SIDS (*but use* sudden infant death syndrome *in first reference*)
siege (*not* -ei-)
sight, sightseeing, sightseer
signal, signalled, signaller
signalman (no abbvn.)
      —Signalman William O'Callaghan
Sikh, the Sikh religion
Siksika (aboriginal band)
silhouette
Silicon Valley
silo, silos
Simoniz (trademark for a car wax)
Sinn Fein
sinus, sinuses
siphon (*not* syphon)

sir, Sir John Jones; Sir John *or preferably* Jones *in second reference*

sirocco (Italian name for Sahara wind)

sitcom (TV situation comedy)

Sitsabaiesan, Rathika (politician)

sizable (*not* -eable)

skating, figure skating, ice skating (*hyphenate when used adjectivally*); *but* speedskating

skeptic, skeptical, skepticism (*not* sc-)

ski, skier, skis, skiing

Ski-Doo (snowmobile trademark)

skid row (*not* road)

skilful

skulduggery

slaughterhouse

Slovakia

small-c conservative

smallmouth (bass)

Smallwood, Joey (*not* Joseph, 1900-1991)

smart-alec

smartphone (*one word*)

Smiths Falls, Ont. (*no apostrophe*)

Smithsonian Institution (*not* Institute)

smoky (*not* smokey)

smorgasbord

smoulder

SMS (for short message service. *Prefer* text message)

snakehead (human smuggler)

SNC-Lavalin Group Inc. (TSX:SNC)

snob, snobbery, snobbish, snobbishness

snow, snowblower, snowboard, snowfall, snowflake, snowflurries, snowstorm

snowbirds (Canadians who winter in the South)

Snowbirds (Canadian Forces flying team)

snowboard cross (*two words*)

snowmobile (*one word*)
snowshoe, snowshoer
s.o.b.
sober
Sobeys Inc., a Sobeys store
Social Crediter (*not* -or)
Social Credit party
socialism, socialist (philosophical attitude)
Socialist (party or member)
Société franco-manitobaine, la
society, Audubon Society
Socred (*n.* and *adj.*)
softpedal (*not* -peddle)
soft-spoken (*hyphen*)
software
softy, softies
Soleil, Le (Quebec)
solicitor general, solicitors general
solo, solos
soluble
Solzhenitsyn, Alexander (1918-2008)
Somali (*n.*), Somalian (*adj.*)
sombre (*not* -er)
some, someday, someplace, somebody, somebodies,
     somehow, someone, something, at some time
     (*two words*), sometime (*adv.; adj.*), somewhat,
     somewhere
Somers, Harry (composer, 1925-99)
somersault
soprano, sopranos
SOS (*no periods*)
Sotheby's Canada Inc.
     —Sotheby's for short
South Asia, South Asian (*not* East India, East Indian)
South Carolina (S.C.)
South Dakota (S.D.)

southeast (*one word*)
    —Southeast Asia (region), southeast Asian
    (*adj.*)
    —Southeast Asia Treaty Organization (SEATO)
Southern Canada, southern Canadian weather
southern France
Southern Hemisphere
southern Ontario
southern states (U.S.)
South Pole, the Pole
sou'wester (waterproof hat)
sovereigntist (*not* sovereignist)
sovereignty-association
Soviet Union, former (Union of Soviet Socialist
    Republics, U.S.S.R.)
soybean, soy sauce
spacewalk
spam (Internet)
Spanish Civil War
spartan
Speaker—Capitalize in all references to avoid
    ambiguity.
    —Speaker Martha Lim, the Speaker
    —deputy Speaker Glenn Eckert, the deputy
    Speaker, former Speaker
Special Investigations Unit (SIU - Ontario)
spectre (*not* -er)
speech from the throne
speedskater, speedskating
spellbinder (*no hyphen*)
spellcheck, spellchecker (*one word*)
sphinx (winged monster)
Sphinx (representation near pyramids)
Spider-Man (comic, movie)
Spielberg, Steven
spina bifida

spinarama (*not* spin-o-rama)
spin off (*v.*), spinoff (*n.* and *adj.*)
splendour
spoonful, spoonfuls
sports writer *(two words)*
sport utility vehicle (*not* sports; SUV)
spring (season)
squadron leader (*no abbvn.*)
Squid-Jiggin' Ground, the (Newfoundland ballad)
Srebrenica (Bosnia)
Sri Lanka, Sri Lankan
    —Sri Lanka Freedom party
SS (steamship)
SS (Schutzstaffel, Nazi elite guard)
St-, Ste-, St.—Use abbreviations in federal and
    provincial names of political ridings. Use St. for
    male and female saints: St. Peter, St. Anne.
stadium, stadiums
staff, staffs (poles), staves (music)
staff inspector, Staff Insp. Albert Dupont
staff sergeant (Staff Sgt.)
Stalin, Josef (1879-1953)
stampede, Calgary Stampede, the Stampede
Standard & Poor's Corp.
    —S&P/TSX composite index
standardbred, thoroughbred
standard time
    —eastern, central, mountain standard time
    —Atlantic, Pacific daylight time
    —MST, EDT (*not* EDST)
stand by (*v.*), standby (*n.*), standbys
stand in (*v.*), stand-in (*n.*)
Standoff, Alta.
stand off (*v.*), standoff (*n.*)
stand out (*v.*), standout (*n.*)
standup (*n.* and *adj.*)

Stanley Cup

Stars and Stripes

startup (*n* and *adj.*)

state, New York state (geog.)

    —State of New York (corp.)

    —*but* in the state of New York

    —state of the union message

Station—Capitalize as important building *but not*
    when known by name of railway or town.

    —Union Station

    —the Via Rail station

    —Mimico station

stationary (not moving)

stationery (writing materials)

Statistics Canada (StatCan, *not* StatsCan, *acceptable
    in headlines*)

St. Bernard (dog)

St. Catharines, Ont.

St. Catharines Standard

STD (*use* sexually transmitted disease)

Ste-Catherine Street (Montreal)

steelworker

Stefansson, Vilhjalmur (explorer, 1879-1962)

Steinem, Gloria (feminist)

Stelco Inc. — now U.S. Steel Canada

stepdaughter, stepson, stepmother, stepfather *but*
    step-parent

Stephenson, Sir William (1896-1989)

stepping-stone (*hyphen*)

Stetson (trademark)

St-Hyacinthe

still life, still lifes

stimulus, stimuli

St. James's Palace (London)

St-Jean, Que.

St-Jean-Baptiste Day (June 24, also Fête nationale)

St. John Ambulance

St. John of Jerusalem, Most Venerable Order of the
Hospital of (usually Order of St. John)

St. John River (N.B.)

St. John's, N.L.

St-Laurent, Louis

St. Lawrence Seaway, the seaway
—St. Lawrence Seaway Authority
—St. Lawrence Seaway Development Corp.
(U.S.)

St. Marguerite Bourgeoys (Canada's first woman
saint, 1620-1700)

St. Martin-in-the-Fields Church (London)
—Academy of St. Martin-in-the-Fields

St. Marys, Ont.

stock exchange, Toronto Stock Exchange

stock market

stockpile (*one word*)

STOL (short takeoff and landing; *avoid*)

Stone Age

Stoney band (Alberta Indians), Stoneys

Stoney Creek, Ont. and N.B.

stony (*not* stoney)

Stony Lake (near Peterborough, Ont.)

Stony Mountain, Man.

Stony Plain, Alta.

Stony Point First Nation (southern Ontario)

storey (building), storeys

storm, hailstorm, rainstorm, snowstorm

storyteller, storytelling

St. Petersburg (formerly Leningrad)

St-Pierre-Miquelon (islands)
—St-Pierre (capital city)

strafe, strafing

Strahl, Chuck (politician)

straightforward (*no hyphen*)

S

Strait—Capitalize when used with names.
　　—Strait of Juan de Fuca
　　—Georgia Strait
straitjacket
straitlaced
stratagem, stratagems
Stratas, Teresa (soprano)
strategic arms limitation talks (SALT)
　　—SALT I, SALT II
Stratford Beacon Herald
Stratford Shakespeare Festival (*formerly* Stratford
　　Festival)
Stratford upon Avon (Britain)
　　—STRATFORD UPON AVON (in placelines)
stratum, strata
streamline (*one word*)
Street—Capitalize when used with names;
　　abbreviate in numbered street addresses.
　　—Bay Street, Wall Street
　　—along Queen Street East
　　—10 Queen St. E.
　　—*but* 10 Downing Street (official residence)
streetcar (*one word*)
Streisand, Barbra
streptococcus, streptococci
　　—*but* strep throat
strikebound (*no hyphen*)
strikebreaker (generally editorial; *use advisedly*)
striptease
strongman
strontium-90
Stroumboulopoulos, George
St. Thomas Times-Journal
St. Valentine's Day, Valentine's Day (Feb. 14)
　　—*but* a valentine (card)
Styrofoam (trademark for a plastic foam)

suave, suavely, suaveness, suavity, suavities
subcommittee (*no hyphen*)
subcompact
sub judice (*two words, but avoid*)
sub-lieutenant (Sub-Lt.)
submachine-gun
subpoena (*n.* and *v.*), subpoenas, subpoenaed,
   subpoenaing
subtle, subtlety, subtleties
subtrade
succinct, succinctly
sudden infant death syndrome (SIDS OK *in second
   reference)*
suffragan (bishop)
suicide (*avoid* 'committed suicide'; *use* 'died by
   suicide,' 'killed himself' *or* 'took her own life')
Sukkot (Jewish festival)
sulfa drugs
sulphide, sulphite, sulphur
Sum 41 (performing group)
summer (season)
summerfallow
Summerside Journal-Pioneer
summit, summit conference (heads of government)
summons, summonses
summonsed (to appear in court)
sun
Suncor Energy Inc. (TSX:SU)
   —Sunoco (retail brand in Canada)
Sunni Muslim
Sunshine List
Super Bowl
supercilious (*not* -silious)
superintendent, Supt. Herman Frank
supermarket (*one word)*
supersede

suppress, suppression, suppressor
supremacist (*not* supremist)
Supreme Court (federal, provincial, state)
Sûreté du Québec (*prefer* Quebec provincial police)
Suriname
SUV (sport utility vehicle)
Suzuki, David (geneticist)
swap (*not* swop)
SWAT (special weapons and tactics) team
sweatshirt
sweepstake
sweeten, sweetener, sweetening
sweetgrass
Sydney, N.S., and Australia, *but* Sidney, B.C.
Sydney Cape Breton Post
Sydney Steel Corp. (Sysco)
syllabus, syllabuses
symbol, symbolize
symmetrical, symmetry
symphony, Tchaikovsky's Fourth Symphony
symposium, symposiums
synagogue, Holy Blossom Synagogue
syndrome, Reye's, Down
synod, Anglican synod, General Synod
      —Lutheran Church
      —Missouri Synod (denom.)
      —Orthodox Holy Synod (Istanbul)
syphilis
Syrah (grape)
syrup (*not* sirup)
Sysco (Sydney Steel Corp.)

T, *as in* to a T
Tabasco (trademark for a hot sauce)
tableau, tableaus
taekwondo (*one word*)
tai chi (*two words*)
Taipei
Tajikistan, Tajik
take off (*v.*), takeoff (*n.*)
take out (*v.*), takeout (*n.*)
take over (*v.*), takeover (*n.*)
Taliban
Tamiflu (trademark for oseltamivir)
tangelo, tangelos
tank, M-60, PT-76, Leopard 1
targeted
tariff, Tariff Act
> —General Agreement on Tariffs and Trade (GATT)

tarsands *(but avoid)*
Taser (trademark — *Use* stun gun for generic reference), Tasered
task force (military term; *avoid overuse*)
tassel, tasselled
tastebuds
tattoo, tattooed
tax-free savings account (TFSA, *but avoid)*
T-ball
T-cell
Tchaikovsky, Peter (1840-1893)
TD Bank Financial Group (Toronto-Dominion Bank and its subsidiaries)
> —TD Canada Trust (banking)
> —TD Waterhouse (investing)

teammate (*no hyphen*)
Teamsters union (*acceptable in all references for* International Brotherhood of Teamsters,

Chauffeurs, Warehousemen and Helpers of America), a teamster (member of the union)

Tea Party (populist political movement in U.S.)

tear gas (*two words*)

technical sergeant (Tech. Sgt.)

Technicolor (trademark for a process of making colour movies)

Teck Cominco Ltd. (TSX:TCK.B)

teenage (*adj.*), teenager, teens

teenybopper

teepee

teetotal, teetotaller, teetotalism

Teflon (trademark for a non-stick coating)

Tehran

telecommunication

Telefilm Canada

Telephone numbers—Use hyphen, not brackets or spaces to break up: 1-519-228-6262, 1-800-268-9237.

TelePrompTer (trademark)

Telex (trade name)

telltale (*no hyphen*)

Telus Corp. (TSX:T)

Temagami, Ont. (*not* Tim-)

Témiscaming, Que. (town)

Témiscamingue (Que. county, electoral district)

temporary foreign workers (lowercase)

Ten Commandments
    —Second Commandment

tendency (*not* -ancy), tendencies

tendon, Achilles tendon, *but* tendinitis

ten-gallon hat

Tennant, Veronica (ballet)

Tennessee (Tenn.)

tenpins (bowling)

tenterhooks (*not* tender-)

Teresa, Mother (1910-1997)
terminus, terminuses
Terry Fox Run
testament, Old Testament
Test match (cricket, rugby)
>—England-Australia Test match
>—the Test
Tetra Pak (cardboard-based packaging)
Texas (*no abbvn.*)
textbook
text message, messaging
thalidomide
Thanksgiving Day (Canada, second Monday in
> October; U.S., last Thursday in November)
the (*lowercase*) Netherlands
>—UTRECHT, Netherlands (placeline)
The—Capitalize at the beginning of the titles of
> books, magazines, movies, TV programs,
> songs, paintings and other compositions. Don't
> capitalize at the start of the names of almanacs,
> the Bible, directories, encyclopedias, gazetteers
> and handbooks.
The Associated Press (AP)
>—The Associated Press says ...
>—*but* the Associated Press reporter
Theatre—Capitalize as important buildings.
>—National Arts Centre
>—Princess of Wales Theatre
theatregoer
The Canadian Press (CP)
>—The Canadian Press says ...
>—*but* the Canadian Press reporter
The Hague
The Pas, Man.
therapeutic

The Royal Canadian Legion
 —the legion announced ...
 —parade of legionnaires
thesis, theses
the West Indies
think tank
Third World (*avoid*; *prefer* developing nations)
Thompson, Greg (politician)
Thomson, R.H. (actor)
Thomson, Tom (painter, 1877-1917)
Thomson Reuters Corp. (TSX:TRI)
 —Thomson, Ken (1923-2006)
thoroughbred, standardbred
Thousand Islands (Ontario)
3D
Three Wise Men
threshold
throne speech, speech from the throne
Thunder Bay Chronicle-Journal
Tiananmen Square
Ticketmaster *but* TicketsNow
tick-tack-toe (game)
tidbit
tie, tying
tiebreaker (game)
tie up (*v.*), tie-up (*n.*)
till, until, *not* 'til
time, daylight, standard
 —eastern daylight time (EDT)
 —Pacific standard time (PST)
 —7 a.m., 6 p.m., 12:30 p.m.
timeline *(one word)*
Time magazine
Times (of London), the
time-slot
Time Warner Inc.

Tim Hortons (*no apostrophe,* TSX:THI)
   —a Tim Hortons shop
Timiskaming (Ontario lake and district)
Timiskaming-Cochrane (federal riding in Ontario)
Timiskaming reserve (Quebec)
Timorese (*n.* and *adj.*)
Titles—Capitalize formal titles when preceding names,
   not when following or when set off by commas:
   Judge John Jones; a judge, John Jones, spoke.
   But lowercase titles used with former, one-time,
   -elect, designate and similar adjectives, as former
   president Bill Clinton, former prime minister Jean
   Chretien, prime minister-designate Julie Smith.
   Lowercase mere occupation (GM president
   John Wong, bus driver Ron Brown) and in sport
   stories (captain Kathleen Keenan).
TiVo (trademark for brand of digital video recorder)
Tkachuk, David (senator)
Tlicho First Nation (Northwest Territories)
TNT (trinitrotoluene)
T.O. (nickname for Toronto)
to a T
toboggan
Toews, Miriam (writer)
Toews, Vic (politician)
tomato, tomatoes
ton (2,000 pounds), long ton (2,240 pounds), tonne
   (1,000 kilograms or 2,204.62 pounds)
   — *Use* ton, not tonne, in colloquial references
   (he weighed a ton; fell like a ton of bricks).
toonie, toonies ($2 coin)
top-notch (*adj.*)
tornado, tornadoes
Toronto Eaton Centre
Toronto St. Michael's Majors (hockey team)

T

Toronto Stock Exchange
    —S&P/TSX composite index
    —TMX Group Inc. (corporation, TSX:X)
    —TSX Venture Exchange
Torstar Corp. (TSX:TS.B)
total, totalled
Touch-Tone (trademark for push-button dialing)
tourniquet
tower, CN Tower, Eiffel Tower
town, Town of Elmira (corp.)
    —*but* in the town of Elmira
township, Wilmot Township
    —*but* in the township of Wilmot
Toys "R" Us
trademark, trade name
traffic, trafficker, trafficking
traitor, traitorous
tranquillity
tranquillizer
TransAlta Corp. (TSX:TA)
transatlantic, transpacific
TransCanada Corp. (TSX:TRP)
    —TransCanada PipeLines Ltd. (TSX:TCA.PR.X)
Trans-Canada Highway
transcontinental (*no hyphen*)
Transcontinental Inc. (TSX:TCL.A)
trans fat (*two words*)
transfer, transferred
transgender (*adj., preferred to* transgendered)
Transkei (former homeland state in South Africa)
translator (*not* -er)
transpacific
Transportation Safety Board
Transport Canada
trauma, traumas, traumatic
travel, traveller, traveller's cheques

Treasury Board, Treasury Board President Tony Clement

treaty, Columbia River Treaty
—Treaty 6 (*not* Six)

Treehouse TV

tremor

trendsetter, trendsetting

Tribune, La (newspaper in Sherbrooke, Que.)

triple-A (bonds, sports leagues)

Triple Crown (horse racing)

triple-decker

Triple-E Senate

TriStar (Lockheed aircraft)

Trivial Pursuit (trademark board game)

Trois-Rivières, Que.

trooper (military, *no abbvn.*), trouper (a staunch colleague — a "real trouper")

Trophy—Capitalize specific names.
—Vézina Trophy
—a championship trophy

Trudeau, Pierre Elliott (1919-2000)

Trudeau, Alexandre (*preferred to* Sacha)

Truman, Harry S. (1884-1972)

trustee, trustee Joanne Rocci

Tsawwassen, B.C.

T-shirt

tsunami (wave), tsunamis *(pl.)*

Tsuu T'ina Nation (aboriginal band)

TSX (Toronto Stock Exchange) (visit tsx.com for updated list of ticker symbols)
—TSX Venture Exchange (junior exchange)
—S&P/TSX composite index

Tube (London subway; also Underground)

tug of war (*no hyphens*)

Tuktoyaktuk, N.W.T.

tumour *but* tumorous

tune-up (*n.*)
tupek (Inuit equivalent of teepee, wigwam)
tuque (knitted cap; otherwise toque)
Turin, Italy
turkey, turkeys
Turkmenistan
Turp, Daniel (politician)
turtleneck sweater (*no hyphen*)
Tussaud's, Madame (wax museum in London)
    —*but* Louis Tussaud's Waxworks (Niagara
    Falls, Ont.)
Tutankhamen
Tutor (training jet)
TVA Group Inc. (TSX:TVA.B)
TV dinner
TV Land (specialty channel)
TVOntario, TVO
tween, tweens (usually eight- to 14-year-olds)
Twelfth Night
Twelve Apostles, the
Twitter, Twittered, Twittering *(uppercase)*
    —tweet *(lowercase)*
two, twos
20th Century Fox *(no hyphen)*
tying (*not* tieing)
typeface
Type 1, Type 2 diabetes
typhoon Alice

U

U-boat
UFO(s) (unidentified flying object(s))
U.K. (*use periods*)
Ukraine (*not* the Ukraine)
Ukrainian
ultimatum, ultimatums
ultra-Orthodox (Jews)
ultrasound
Ultrasuede (trademark for a mock suede)
ultra vires (beyond the powers, *but avoid*)
umiak (Inuit open boat)
Umlaut—Indicate in German names by placing
    letter "e" after vowel affected.
    —Goebbels for Göbbels
    —Duesseldorf for Düsseldorf
unabomber (Theodore Kaczynski)
unchristian, *but* non-Christian
unco-operative
unco-ordinated
underprivileged
undersecretary (*one word*)
underway
unforeseen
unforgivable (*not* -eable)
UNICEF *(OK in first reference)*
uninterested (not interested), disinterested
    (impartial)
union, state of the union message
Union Jack
Union Nationale
Union of Soviet Socialist Republics, former (U.S.S.R.,
    Soviet Union)
United Appeal campaign
United Church of Canada

U

United Kingdom—England, Scotland, Wales and Northern Ireland. But use "British government" and such in preference to "United Kingdom government."

-U.K. *(periods)*

United Nations (UN)

—Food and Agriculture Organization of the United Nations (FAO, *but avoid*)

—General Assembly

—International Bank for Reconstruction and Development (World Bank)

—International Civil Aviation Organization (ICAO)

—International Court of Justice (*no abbvn.*)

—International Labour Organization (ILO)

—International Monetary Fund (IMF)

—Office for the Co-ordination of Humanitarian Affairs (OCHA, *but avoid*)

—Security Council

—UN Children's Fund (UNICEF)

—UN Educational, Scientific and Cultural Organization (UNESCO)

—UN High Commissioner for Refugees

—World Food Program

—World Health Organization (WHO)

University—Capitalize the names of universities and colleges.

—Memorial University

—Simon Fraser University

—Regis College

Lowercase departments, programs and courses.

—political science department

—native studies course

—faculty of education

Unknown Soldier

unmistakable (*not* -eable)
unshakable (*not* -eable)
unwieldy
Upper Canada (region; name for Ontario 1791-1841)
uppercase (*n.* and *v.*)
upper house, chamber
Upstate New York
Uranium One Inc. (TSX: UUU)
URL (uniform or universal resource locator)
US (use only with dollar figures: US$550)
usable (*not* useable)
usage (*not* useage)
US Airways
USA Today
U.S. Steel Canada (formerly Stelco Inc.)
usurer, usurious, usury
Utah (no abbvn.)
U-turn
Uzbekistan, Uzbek (*n.* and *adj.*)

V

vacillate

vacuum

Val-d'Isère

Vale (formerly Vale Inco)

valentine (card)
    —*but* Valentine's Day

Valhalla

Valium (trademark for a tranquillizer)

Valkyrie

valley, Fraser Valley

valour *but* valorous

Van, Von—When lowercase in names, capitalize
    only at start of sentences. Van in Vietnamese
    names is uppercase.

Vancouver Grizzlies (former basketball team)

Van Doo (nickname of Quebec's Royal 22e
    Regiment)
    —Van Doos (personnel of the regiment)
    —Van Doo (one member)

van Gogh, Vincent (1853-1890)

Vanier, Georges (1888-1967)

VANOC (organizing committee for the Vancouver
    2010 Olympics)

vape, vaping, vape shop, vape pen

vapour, vapourish *but* vaporous, vaporize

Vaseline (trademark for a petroleum jelly)

Vatican II, Second Vatican Council

vaudeville

V-chip (television)

VCR (videocassette recorder)

Veda (scripture of Hinduism)

VE-Day, VJ-Day (for Victory in Europe Day, Victory
    in Japan Day)

Velcro (trademark)

venetian blind

ventilator (*not* respirator)

veranda (*not* -ah)

verbatim (*not* -um)

Vermilion, Alta.

Vermont (Vt.)

versus—Use the abbreviation vs. only in sports schedules, agate and the names of court cases.

vertebra, vertebrae

Veterans Affairs Canada (*no apostrophe*)

veterinarian

Vézina Trophy

Viagra (impotence drug)

Via Rail (*not* VIA)

vice (bad habit), vise (clamp)

vice-admiral (*no abbvn.*)

vice-president

—U.S. Vice-President James Smith

—former U.S. vice-president Al Gore

—GM vice-president Joan Arthur

vice versa (*two words*)

vichyssoise

vicious

Vickers, Jon (tenor)

Victoria Cross (VC)

Victoria Times Colonist

vidalia onion

video, videocassette, videocassette recorder (VCR), videotape, video game

Videotron (cable provider owned by Quebecor Inc.)

vie, *but* vying

Vietnam, Vietnamese

vigour, vigorous

vilify

village, Village of Bridgeport (corp.)

—*but* in the village of Bridgeport

VIP (for very important person), VIPs

Virgin (Christ's mother)

Virginia (Va.)

Virgin Islands (*no abbvn.*)

virtuoso, virtuosos

Visa (credit card)

vis-a-vis

viscount, Viscount Montgomery

viscous (sticky)

vise (clamp), vice (bad habit)

Vishnu

VisionTV (specialty channel)

vitamin B, B-12

Vizinczey, Stephen (novelist)

VJ (*not* veejay), VJs, VJing

VLT (video lottery terminal)

V-neck

vociferous

voice mail (*two words*)

Voice of Women (VoW)

voice-over-Internet protocol (VoIP *in second
        reference)*

Voisey's Bay (Labrador)

Voix de l'Est, La (newspaper in Granby, Que.)

volatile

volcano, volcanoes

Volkswagen

vomit, vomited, vomiting

Von, Van—When lowercase in names, capitalize
        only at start of sentence except for van in
        Vietnamese names, which is uppercase.
        —Kai-Uwe von Hassel (Germany)
        —Nguyen Van Hai (Vietnam)

vow (solemn oath; often misused)

vs. (abbreviation for versus, used only in sports
        schedules, agate and the names of court cases)

wacky (*not* whacky)

wagon, bandwagon, chuckwagon, station wagon

wake-up call

Walesa, Lech

walkie-talkie

Walkman (trademark for headset stereo)

walk out (*v.*), walkout (*n.*)

Walkuere, Die (Wagner opera)

wall, Berlin Wall, Great Wall of China, Wailing Wall
(in Jerusalem; *prefer* Western Wall), Wall Street

Walmart

—Walmart (brand name)

—Walmart Canada

—Wal-Mart Stores Inc. (U.S. corporate entity)

War—Capitalize major armed conflicts.

—Civil War (U.S.)

—First World War (*not* World War I)

—Persian Gulf War

—Second World War (*not* World War II)

—*but* a third world war

—Six-Day War

—Korean War

—Vietnam War

—Wars of the Roses

—cod war

—tariff war

—Cold War (fanciful term)

Ward 2

warhorse, warlord, warmonger

Warner Bros. Entertainment (division of AOL Time
Warner)

warrant officer (*no abbvn.*)

—chief warrant officer

—master warrant officer

Warsaw Pact, former

wartime

Washington (Wash.)

Washington, D.C.

WASP (white Anglo-Saxon Protestant)

Wassermann test

wastebasket

Wasylycia-Leis, Judy (politician)

watchdog

waterfowl

Waterloo, University of (*not* Waterloo University)

Waterloo Region Record; the Record, of Waterloo
Region

water-ski, water-skiing

wavelength

web, web browser, webcam, webcast, web-enabled,
webmaster, web page, web server, website but
World Wide Web

Web Addresses—It is not necessary to include
http://. But do include less familiar common
forms such as ftp://. Follow upper and
lowercase: www.thecanadianpress.com.
When a company uses its web address as
its corporate name, capitalize the first letter:
Amazon.com.

Week—Capitalize special events: Earth Week.

weekday, weekend, weeklong (*one word*)

weird, weirdo

Welch (regiment names)
—*but* Welsh Guards

Welland Canal

well-being (*hyphen*)

Welsh (folk, tongue)

welsh (on a bet; *avoid*)

Welshpool, N.B. (*not* Welch-)

West—Capitalize regions but not their derivatives.
Lowercase mere direction or position.
—the West (region of Canada or the world)

—the richest countries in the West
—the richest western countries
—The West won the Grey Cup.
—a westerner
—one western MP
—Western Canada
—a western Canadian
—the western Canadian provinces
—the western provinces
—western premiers
—in western Manitoba
—The snow moved west across Western Canada.
—West Coast (region)
—west coast (shoreline)
—the East-West talks
—western Europe
—western leaders
—western France
—Western Hemisphere

West Bank (of the River Jordan)
West End (London theatre district)
western (movie, book)
Western University, Western (*prefer to official name*, University of Western Ontario)
WestJet Airlines Ltd. (TSX:WJA)
Westminster, Westminster Abbey (London), New Westminster, B.C.
Westmorland County (N.B. and England)
West Nile virus
Weston, Hilary
West Virginia (W.Va.)
Weyerhaeuser Co. Ltd.
W-Five
whack (to strike)
wharf, wharfs

Wheat—Capitalize varieties generally except where usage has established the lowercase; Selkirk, *but* durum.

wheelchair

whereabouts (usually takes a singular verb)

Whibley, Deryck (Sum 41)

whip, party whip John O'Neill

whiskey (Irish and American); whisky (Scottish and Canadian); whiskies

whistleblower *(no hyphen)*

whiteboard

Whitehorse, Yukon

White House

white paper (a report issued by government to provide information)

whiz, whiz-kid

whodunit (*not* -nn-)

Whycocomagh (First Nations band on Cape Breton)

wide (*suffix*), citywide, worldwide, provincewide, countrywide (*avoid* nationwide when countrywide is meant), Canada-wide

widescreen

wield

wiener, wiener schnitzel

Wi-Fi (wireless fidelity; prefer description such as wireless network *in first reference*)

wigwag (*no hyphen*)

Wi-LAN Inc. (TSX:WIN)

Wildrose (formerly Wildrose Alliance)
      — Wildrose party, Wildrose member
      — Wildrose Party of Alberta (official name)

Wild West

Wilfrid Laurier University

wilful (*not* willful)

Wimbledon tennis championships

wind chill (*two words*)

wing commander (Wing Cmdr.)

winter (season)

Winter Olympic Games, the Winter Games, the
Games

Wisconsin (Wis.)

wit, halfwit, halfwitted
—at his wit's end

withdraw, withdrawal

withhold

W Network (TV)

Wojtyla, Karol (Pope John Paul II, 1978-2005)

Woman—Don't use as an adjective unless
man would be used in similar fashion
(womenswear, menswear). *Prefer* female if it is
necessary to specify sex.
—female astronaut, *not* woman astronaut

Woman's Christian Temperance Union (*not*
Women's)

womenswear, menswear

woollen, woolly

Workers' Compensation, Health and Safety Board
(Yukon)

Workers' Compensation Board (*with apostrophe* in
Alberta, British Columbia, Northwest Territories
and Nunavut, Nova Scotia, Saskatchewan)

Workers Compensation Board (*no apostrophe* in
Manitoba, Prince Edward Island)

workforce

workload

workplace

Workplace Health, Safety and Compensation
Commission (New Brunswick, Newfoundland
and Labrador)

Workplace Safety and Insurance Board (Ontario)

work-to-rule campaign

world
>—Old World, New World
>—free world (*but avoid*)
>—Third World

World Bank

World Cup (soccer)

World Health Organization (WHO)

World Series (baseball), the Series

world's fair, Montreal, New York
>—Expo 67, Expo 86 (*no apostrophe*)

World Trade Center (New York)

worldwide (*one word*)

World Wide Web, the web

World Wildlife Fund (*not* federation)

worshippers

worthwhile

write down (*v.*), writedown (*n.*)

write off (*v.*), writeoff (*n.*)

wrongdoer, wrongdoing, wrongful

Wrzesnewskyj, Borys (politician)

Wyoming (Wyo.)

X-Y-Z

X-Acto (trademark for knives)
Xbox
X chromosome, Y chromosome
Xerox (trademark for a photocopier, etc.)
X-Files, The
Xinhua News Agency (official agency of Chinese
      government)
X-rated (movie)
X-ray (*n.* and *v.*)
Xstrata Nickel (formerly Falconbridge; now division
      of Xstrata PLC)
yahoo
Yahoo Inc. (*not* Yahoo! Inc.)
Yahweh
Yamani, Sheik Ahmed Zaki
Yangon (formerly Rangoon)
Yankee
yarmulke (skullcap)
Year, Man of the, Newsmaker of the
Yellowhead Pass
yenta
Y-Flyer (sailboat)
YMCA (Young Men's Christian Association)
yogurt
Yom Kippur
Youth Criminal Justice Act (replaced Young
      Offenders Act (*no apostrophe)* in April 2003)
YouTube
yo-yo, yo-yos
Yukon (*no abbvn.*)
yule, yuletide
yuppie (young urban professional)
YWCA (Young Women's Christian Association)
Zaire (now Congo)
Zamboni (trademark for ice-surfacing machine)
Zellers (*no apostrophe*)

X-Y-Z

Zen Buddhism
zero, zeros
Zhou Enlai (1898-1976, formerly Chou En-lai)
zidovudine (HIV-AIDS drug, also called AZT)
zigzag (*no hyphen*)
Zimbabwe
Zinfandel
Zion, Zionism, Zionist
zip code (U.S.)
zip line
Znaimer, Moses (television)
zodiac
zoologist, zoology
zucchini

Numbers

'60s Scoop
Act 1, the first act
Article 8, Art. 8
behind the 8-ball
C (used only with dollar figures: C$1,386)
Category 3
CBC Radio One, Radio Two
Cell Block 5
cents, nine cents, 43 cents
Channel 2 (television)
Chapter 2
Chemical elements—Write out *in first reference* (carbon dioxide) but symbols *OK in second reference* if popularly used: CO_2.
Chromosome 7
Cloud 9
Day 1
Detroit Three automakers
55 BC; AD 1978
four-by-four (four-wheel-drive vehicle)
4-for-5 (four hits in five at-bats)
4-H
49th parallel
4-20 (for April 20 'Weed Day')
Fractions—Use figures for all numbers with fractions (9 3/4). Spell out and hyphenate common fractions used alone (three-quarters).
Grade 7
G7, G8 (group of countries)
karat, 14-karat gold
Latitude, Longitude—44 degrees north, 49 degrees 30 minutes west, etc.
Leopard 1 (tank)
line 46
911 (emergency calls), 9/11 (for day of terrorist attacks in United States)

Numbers

1930s, '30s
> —*but* Expo 67, Expo 86 (*no apostrophe*)

1920-21, *but* 1999-2003

No. 1, number 1 (*not* number one)

10 Downing Street (*exception*)

10th (*no period*)

page 23, p. 23

paragraph 3

Phase 1 (drug trials, etc.)

Room 14

Scene 3, the third scene

season 2

Section 8, Sec. 8

7Up (soft drink)

Telephone numbers—Use hyphens, not spaces
> or brackets to break up: 416-228-6262,
> 1-888-268-9237.

3D

Treaty 6

24-7 (24 hours a day, seven days a week, *but avoid*)

24 Sussex Drive (*exception*)

2,4-D (weed killer)

two-by-four

20-something, 30-something

20th century

20th Century Fox

US (used only with dollar figures: US$295)

verse 3

VIII (*no period*)

V-6, V-8 (engine)

Plain Words

When there is a choice of words, prefer the short to the long, the familiar to the unfamiliar. This chapter lists some long or formal words along with some shorter or more familiar alternatives that may do the job better.

abandon	leave, quit, give up
abbreviate	shorten, cut
abduct	kidnap, seize
abolish	end, do away with, scrap
abrasion	scrape, scratch
accelerate	hurry, speed up
accessible	easily reached, ready, at hand
accommodate	house, shelter, put up
accordingly	so, therefore
according to	under; say
accumulate	pile up, collect
acknowledge	admit, concede
acquire	buy, gain, get
acquit	free, clear, release
additional	added, more, extra
in addition to	besides
adhere	stick, cling
adjacent	beside, next to, touching
administer	manage, direct, control
adverse	harmful, damaging
advise	tell, write, inform
advocate	support, call for
affluent	rich, well-to-do
aggravate	annoy, provoke, worsen
aggressive	pushing, pushy
alienate	put off, turn against
allegiance	loyalty
alleviate	ease, soften
alteration	change, revision
alternate	take turns

Plain Words

alternative	choice, other
amalgamate	unite, combine
amendment	change, revision
amicable	friendly, pleasant
anonymous	nameless, unknown
antagonize	offend, anger
apparent	clear, plain, obvious
appreciative	grateful, thankful
appropriate	fit, proper
approximately	about
aptitude	gift, knack, talent
arguably	perhaps, maybe
as far as... is concerned	as to
asphyxiate	choke, suffocate
assist	help, aid
astute	shrewd, clever
attempt	try
attired	dressed, wearing
authentic	genuine, real, true
authorize	approve, allow, give power
autonomous	free, independent, self-governing
available	ready, on hand
bargain	deal
beneficial	good for, helpful, useful
bereavement	death, loss
beverage	drink
biannual	twice a year, every two years
bigotry	bias, narrow-mindedness, racism
bilateral	two-sided
bona fide	real, in good faith
capacity	ability, position, space, size
catastrophe	disaster
cease	stop, end
censure	blame, scold
characteristic	trait, mark, feature
circumstance	event, condition, fact

Plain Words

clad	dressed, wearing
coagulate	clot, congeal
coerce	force, press
collaborate	work together, team up
comatose	unconscious
commence	begin, start
commitment	promise, pledge
communicable	catching, infectious
communicate	tell, inform, write, telephone
comparable	like, similar
compensate	pay, make up
competent	able, trained
complete	fill out, finish
complimentary	free
comply	follow, obey, give in
compulsion	urge
conceive	think up, imagine, dream up
concerning	about, for, on
conclude	end
concur	agree, match
conduct	carry on, do, run
confederation	alliance, league, union
congenital	inborn, inbred
conscientious	careful, painstaking
consequently	so
considerable	much, ample
consolation	comfort, relief, help
conspicuous	plain, obvious
constitute	are, make up, form
construct	build, make
consult	ask, talk over
consume	eat, use up
contaminate	taint, pollute, dirty, poison
contemplate	consider, study, weigh
contribute	give, share, help
controversy	debate, issue

Plain Words

contusion	bruise
convenient	useful, handy
convulsion	seizure, spasm
corroborate	confirm, verify
counterfeit	false, phoney, fake
courteous	polite
criterion	test, rule, model, yardstick
currently	now
deactivate	shut off, close
dearth	lack, shortage, scarcity
deceased	dead
decompose	rot, decay
decontaminate	purify, disinfect, sterilize
decrease	cut, drop, fall
decry	blame, condemn
de-emphasize	play down, softpedal
de facto	actual, real
defective	faulty, broken
deficient	lacking, poor
defraud	cheat, swindle, fleece
demonstrate	show, prove
depart	go, leave, check out
deplete	empty, sap, reduce
depreciate	lessen, cheapen, scorn
depressed	backward, diminished, sad
designate	name, call, label
destitute	poor, needy, bare
determine	fix, test, find out, decide, settle
development	growth, change
deviate	swerve, stray, turn aside, vary
dimension	size
diminutive	tiny
disallow	turn down, reject
discontinue	end, give up, stop
disembark	get off, leave, land
disguise	hide, mask

Plain Words

disintegrate	fall apart, crumble, break up
dispatch	send, issue
display	show, bare
distinguish	tell apart, make out
distribute	hand out, spread
divulge	tell, give, reveal
don	put on, get into
donation	gift, present
draconian	harsh
dubious	unsure, doubtful
duplicate	copy, repeat
dwell	live, occupy
eccentric	odd, strange
economical	thrifty, cheap
edifice	building
elevate	lift, raise
eliminate	get rid of, throw out, drop
emaciated	gaunt, bony, thin, wasted
eminent	famous, high, noted
emphasize	stress, underline
empirical	practical
employ	use, hire, apply
encounter	meet, come upon
endorsement	support, backing
enhance	add to, improve
ensue	follow, develop
enumerate	count, add up, cite
envisage	see, foresee, imagine
escalate	step up, intensify
eschew	avoid
in the event of	if
evident	plain, obvious
excessive	too much, undue
in excess of	over
exhibit	show, reveal, display
exonerate	free, clear, acquit

Plain Words

exorbitant	excessive, too high, overpriced
expedite	speed up, push
expenditure	spending, expense, cost
experience	feel, live through, undergo
expertise	skill, knowledge, know-how
explicit	clear, precise, exact
extended	long, drawn out
extensive	large, wide, broad, roomy
exterminate	wipe out, destroy
extinguish	put out, douse, smother
fabricate	make, build; lie, trump up
facilitate	ease, make easy, help, lighten
failed to	did not
fallacy	error, fault, pitfall
feasible	possible, can be done, workable
finalize	finish, complete, end
fluctuate	rise and fall, swing, waver
fortunate	lucky, happy
fracture	break
frequently	often
frustration	defeat, dismay
fundamental	basic, real
generate	produce, cause
gratuity	gift, tip
on the grounds that	because
hazardous	unsafe, risky, dangerous
ideology	beliefs
illumination	light, insight
illustration	example, picture, drawing
immediately	at once, now
immense	huge, vast
immovable	set, firm, fixed
impartial	neutral, fair, just
impeccable	flawless, perfect
impede	slow, hamper, stall, hinder
imperative	urgent, vital, pressing

Plain Words

imperceptible	slight, subtle, hidden
impersonate	copy, mimic
impetus	spur, push, urge
implement	do, set up, begin, carry out
impolite	rude
impostor	cheat, fraud, ringer
impotent	weak, helpless, powerless
inaccuracy	mistake, error
inadvertent	accidental, careless
inadvisable	unwise, risky
inaugurate	begin, launch
in camera	private
incapacitate	disable, damage, lay up
incarcerate	jail, intern, imprison
incision	cut, slit
incite	rouse, prod, goad
inclement	stormy, harsh, nasty
incompetent	unfit, inept
inconceivable	incredible, beyond belief
incorrect	wrong
increase	rise, go up, gain, grow
incredulous	dubious, skeptical
indefinite	vague, uncertain, dim
independent	free; well-off
indicate	show, suggest, hint, imply
indigenous	native
indignant	angry, upset
indispensable	vital, crucial, essential
individual	person, man, woman
ineligible	unfit, unsuitable
inevitable	sure, destined
inexpensive	cheap, low-priced, modest
inflexible	rigid, firm, stiff
inform	tell
ingenious	clever, deft, masterly
inherent	inborn, inbred, essential

Plain Words

inhibit	check, hinder, curb
initial	first
initiate	begin, open
injunction	ban, order
in lieu of	instead of
innate	inborn, natural
innovation	change, novelty
input	say, opinion, suggestion
inquire	ask
insecure	unsafe, unsure
institute	set up, begin, found
instrument	tool, agent, means
insufficient	not enough, short
insurrection	revolt, riot, mutiny
integrate	absorb, combine, mix
intention	aim, plan, goal, purpose
interface	work together, connect
intermission	pause, break
interrogate	question, pump, quiz
interrupt	break in, butt in, hinder, stop
intersection	corner
inundate	flood, deluge, overflow, engulf
irrelevant	beside the point, off-base
irresponsible	careless, rash, reckless
jurisdiction	control, power, domain
laceration	cut, tear, gash
latitude	scope, range
laud	praise
lenient	mild, gentle, sparing
liberate	free, rescue
locality	place, spot, site
locate	find, pinpoint
lubricate	oil, grease
magnitude	size, extent
majority	most, bulk, mass
manufacture	make, produce, build

Plain Words

maximum	most, biggest, longest
meaningful	big, important, significant
medication	medicine, remedy, pill, drug
mediocre	ordinary, run-of-the-mill
mentality	mind, frame of mind, outlook
methodology	method
milieu	setting, scene; culture
minimal	small, token
minimize	lessen, play down, belittle, diminish
minuscule	tiny
mitigate	ease, soften, make mild, temper
modification	change
momentous	important
motivate	inspire, drive, cause
narrate	tell, recount, relate
nauseous	sickening, repulsive
necessitate	need, compel, call for
negligent	careless
negotiate	bargain, talk business
neo-natal	newborn
neophyte	novice, beginner, learner, apprentice
neutralize	offset, cancel
nominal	small, token
notification	notice, warning
numerous	many
nurture	feed, train
nutritious	nourishing, wholesome
objective	end, aim, goal, mission
obligation	duty, debt
oblige	compel, force
obscure	dim, hidden
observation	remark, comment
obsolescent	dying out, disappearing
obsolete	worn-out, disused, out-of-date
obstruction	barrier, block, hurdle
obtain	get, come by, gain

Plain Words

occasion	event, cause, chance
occupation	job, trade, profession
occurrence	event, incident
ongoing	continuing, active, permanent
operate	work, run; cut out, remove
opportunity	chance
optimal	best
option	choice
originate	invent, create
outrageous	shocking, disgusting
overabundance	abundance, excess, glut
overview	view, survey
palatable	tasty, pleasing, sweet
panache	dash, pizzazz, zip
parameter	limit, boundary
paraphrase	reword, restate
parochial	narrow
participate	take part, share in, join in
pending	until, in the air
perceive	see, view, regard
periphery	edge, outskirts
permanent	lasting, endless
permission	consent, go-ahead
perquisite	perk, fringe benefit, right
persevere	persist, hold on, endure, stand
perspiration	sweat
persuade	win over, sway, coax
pertinent	fit, right, apt
philosophy	idea, view, system
physician	doctor
place	put
pollute	dirty, poison, taint
portion	part, piece, share
position	job
possess	own, have
postpone	put off, shelve, delay

practicable	workable, can be done
pragmatic	practical
preclude	prevent, shut out, avert
predicament	difficulty
prejudicial	harmful
preliminary to	before
preparedness	readiness
prerogative	privilege, right
presently	soon
prestigious	honoured, famous
principal	main, chief
prior to	before
probability	likelihood, chance
procedure	way, course, method
proceed	go
proficient	skilled, deft, masterly
prohibit	ban, prevent, forbid
project	plan
proliferation	spread
prophesy	foretell, predict
proponent	advocate, supporter
proposal	plan, offer
prosthesis	artificial limb
protocol	etiquette, usage
provide	give, offer, have, say
proviso	condition
provoke	stir up, annoy, tease
prowess	skill, talent
purchase	buy
for the purpose of	to
qualification	ability, skill, requirement
quandary	difficulty, impasse
radiant	bright, glowing
rampant	rife, raging, unchecked
ratification	assent, acceptance, approval
rationale	reason, thinking, theory

Plain Words

reciprocate	return, share
reconnaissance	survey, scrutiny
recuperate	recover, get well, rally
reduction	cut
redundant	extra, not needed
with regard to	on, about, as to
regimen	rule, system; diet
regret	be sorry
regulation	rule, law, bylaw
rehabilitate	redeem, straighten out, restore
reimburse	pay back, refund
reinforce	strengthen, brace, prop up
reiterate	repeat, say again
remainder	rest, others
remark	say
renegade	outlaw, crook, criminal
replica	copy, model
representative	agent, deputy
reprimand	rebuke, scold
repudiate	disown, reject, deny
require	need, call for, ask for
rescind	set aside, repeal, cancel
resemblance	likeness
reside	live, occupy, room
residence	house, home, apartment
respond	answer, reply
restrain	check, stop
retain	keep
retrench	cut down, reduce
retrieve	bring back, recover
reveal	show
rupture	break, snap
sanguine	optimistic, confident
sanitary	healthful, clean, germ-free
saturate	soak, fill, drench
segment	part

Plain Words

selection	choice, pick
self-confessed	confessed
significant	serious, grave
similar	like
situated	placed, put, housed
socialize	mingle, meet, make friends
solicit	ask for, beg, canvass
spacious	vast, roomy
state	say
stigma	stain, taint, disgrace
stimulate	arouse, stir up, excite
stringent	strict, tight
submit	give, send
subordinate	helper, assistant
subsequently	later, after that
substantiate	prove, support, back up
sufficient	enough, plenty, ample
suffocate	smother, choke
summon	send for
superficial	shallow, slight, flimsy
supersede	replace, displace
in short supply	scarce
supportive of	support
sustain	suffer, bear
syndrome	symptoms, clue
systematic	orderly, regular
technicality	detail, minor point
temperamental	moody, fickle, high-strung
terminal	fatal
terminate	end, stop
therapeutic	healing
toxic	poisonous, deadly
transform	change, alter
transmit	send
transparent	clear, lucid
traumatic	shocking

Plain Words

turbulent	stormy, wild, violent
ulterior	hidden
ultimate	last, final
underprivileged	poor, hard up
unfavourable	harmful, damaging
unmistakable	clear, plain, evident
unpretentious	modest, humble
unveil	announce
updated	current
upgrade	improve, better
urbane	polished, well-bred, elegant
utilize	use
vacillate	waver, falter, hesitate
validity	truth, proof
vaunted	celebrated, famous
vehicle	car, truck, bus
velocity	speed
venue	place, site
verbatim	word for word, exactly
viable	workable, practical, usable
vicinity	near, close
visualize	see, foresee, imagine, picture
vulnerable	defenceless
withhold	hold back, refuse
withstand	bear, endure, resist, cope

Other books

The Canadian Press Stylebook
The Canadian Press Stylebook is the bible consulted by journalists at Canada's national news agency as they deliver hundreds of stories each day to newspapers, broadcasters and Internet sites. The Stylebook is a one-stop reference guide for writing cleanly, accurately and concisely. It includes:

• Easy-to-follow guidelines on capitalization, punctuation, abbreviations and other writing style and editing issues.
• Chapters on the basics of being a journalist, including reporting, handling breaking news, interviewing techniques, political reporting, headline writing and more.
• A chapter on writing for and about the Internet
• A chapter on public relations and the media, including advice on planning and writing press releases, holding news conferences and working with the media.
• Current listings and spellings on countries and cities around the world and a pronunciation guide to Canadian place names
• Up-to-date information on changes to Canada's laws on polls, elections and youth justice.
• Current advice on how to use access-to-information laws.
• Detailed advice on writing and editing for broadcast, dealing with the spoken word and video.

To order:
Visit thecanadianpress.com/books,
email stylebooks@thecanadianpress.com
or call 416-507-2197.

Other books

Web-based, fully searchable edition of the Stylebook and Caps and Spelling now available
All the authoritative advice on writing and editing you expect from The Canadian Press is now conveniently available at the click of a mouse through your own password-protected online account. If you prefer to use a search engine that quickly finds the content you need, instead of thumbing through an index, turn to the online stylebooks. If, instead of writing in the margins or attaching sticky notes, you prefer to create an online, searchable archive of your own notes, examples, style entries and commonly misspelled words, the online stylebooks are for you.
The stylebooks will continue to be published for hard-copy lovers, while online subscribers will benefit from:

• The convenience of using their writing resource from anywhere they have Internet access.
• The speed of real-time updates and email notifications of all style changes or additional content made by the editor of the stylebooks. No more waiting for the next edition to be printed!
• The flexibility of using the basic and advanced search tools or using the intuitive links organized by popular topics, by chapter and by new entries and recent changes to the stylebooks.
• The power of searching a growing database of frequently asked questions and answers or submitting a style question directly to the editor of the stylebooks.

To sign up for an annual subscription for one or more users within your organization:
Visit thecanadianpress.com/books,
email onlinestylebooks@thecanadianpress.com
or call 416-507-2197.

Guide de rédaction – Award-winning guide for
French-language writers

Winner of a prestigious award from the Office
québécois de la langue française, this fifth edition –
the first in almost 15 years – features:

• easy-to-follow rules for finding the right
expressions and handling typographic and linguistic
difficulties
• a glossary of terms and concepts in finance, law,
sports and labour relations
• lists of troublesome words and common mistakes
to avoid
• sections on writing about terrorism and the
Canadian military
• advice on writing for and about the Internet.

To order:
Visit thecanadianpress.com/books,
email stylebooks@thecanadianpress.com
or call 416-507-2197.

Notes